ATTENTION
and
HUMAN
PERFORMANCE

Steven W. Keele
University of Oregon

Goodyear Publishing Company, Inc.
Pacific Palisades, California

Copyright © 1973 by

GOODYEAR PUBLISHING COMPANY, INC.

Pacific Palisades, California

Current printing (last digit):

10 9 8 7 6 5 4 3 2 1

Library of Congress Catalog Card Number: 72-84006

ISBN: 0-87620-042-0

Y-0420-3

Printed in the United States of America

 **CONTENTS**

 **PREFACE**

The psychological processes underlying human performance are enormously complex. At a broad level, three major divisions in the processes mediating performance can be made—storage of information in memory, retrieval of stored information, and the application of mental operations or overt movements to the retrieved information. Within each of these broad divisions, however, myriad issues arise. Memory storage is not a simple, unitary process. Information may be represented in many modes; transformations may occur between modes; and some representations may be more or less persistent over time as compared to others. Furthermore, many questions arise regarding the conditions under which information becomes stored. Can learning occur during sleep? Is repetition sufficient for storage? How does imagery affect recall? Similarly, a large number of factors influence memory retrieval and movement. Cutting across each of these issues are considerations of attention. We want to know which of the subprocesses require attention and which do not. In addition, we want to develop, if possible, a general theory of attention that covers all three of the major divisions of information processing.

This book introduces some facts and theories about the information processes underlying human performance. Although the book is introductory, it is not elementary. It is intended to serve several levels of readers, from the beginning reader of psychology to the more advanced reader not thoroughly familiar with information processing. Because the book is introductory it is selective. The particular studies discussed were chosen because they develop central concepts of attention and human performance. Some important topics, such as statistical decision theory, are treated minimally because of space limitations.

Many people have aided me in the preparation of this book, by giving me encouragement, ideas, and criticism. I appreciate very much the comments and suggestions of Jerry Ells, Douglas Hintzman, Richard Huggins, Beth Kerr, Donald Norman, Michael Posner, Harvey Rogers, Mary Rothbart, Jock Schwank, Terry Templeman, and James Voss. I thank Karen Evans, Betty Jean Keele, Jody Robinson, and Karen Slye for their extensive work on producing the manuscript. My research activities, much of which contributed to this book, were supported by the Advanced Research Projects Agency of the Department of Defense, monitored by the Air Force Office of Scientific Research (Contract No. F 44620-67-C-0009). Special thanks are due to Ray Hyman who was principal investigator of this group research project. Support was also provided by a National Science Foundation Grant (GB 21020).

 Chapter 1

HUMAN INFORMATION PROCESSING

People, like other organisms, are in constant interaction with their environments. Changes occur in their environments and people react so as to adapt to the changes. Many of these reactions are determined to a large extent by the genetic inheritance of man. Blinking, sucking reflexes, and vasomotor responses to temperature change are examples of inherited adaptive reactions. Other adaptive responses are the result of learning. Out of a range of possible responses to a particular situation, an individual may find that some are more effective than others. When a similar situation later arises, the more effective responses are then produced and are said to be learned behaviors.

For man, the processes intervening between an environmental stimulus and his subsequent response may be quite complex. A dog, when initially commanded to bark, may not in fact bark for some time. When the dog finally does bark following the command, it is given food or some other reward. After the procedure has been repeated a number of times, the command will elicit the desired response, and the dog is said to have learned to bark on command. For such learning to occur, the command, the response, and the reward must be closely contiguous. In humans, learning often occurs without contiguity between the environmental stimulus and the behavioral response. You may read a favorable newspaper review about a play and give no particular response at the time. A day or a month later, you may learn that the play is at your favorite theater, remember that it has a good rating, and decide to attend it. There is no contiguity between your original reading of the newspaper and your ultimate behavior. Information obtained from the reading is stored for later use. Under appropriate conditions, stored information is retrieved and combined with other information from the environment, and at that time some behavior occurs.

The notion of a memory system is useful to account for the frequent lack of contiguity between an environmental event and a person's reaction to it. Indeed, there may be no reaction until some subsequent event occurs, and information derived from the two events is combined. The combining of information derived from two events widely separated in time implies that the earlier information was *stored*. Stored information is of no use, however, unless it is retrievable. Memory *retrieval* is thus the second major process inferred. Retrieved information can be operated on in a variety of ways. It may be rehearsed for more permanent storage, as when you remind yourself that an errand must be performed. It may be combined with other, current information and then stored, as when you mentally update your checkbook. It may be utilized in a memory search for other relevant information, as when you are reminded of a dinner date and search your memory for the address. Eventually, however, adaptation to the environment requires an appropriate response, usually in the form of movement. The end product of memory retrieval, therefore, is *movement*.

Input from environmental events—be they changes in light patterns or auditory patterns, or external forces exerted on the organism, such as written, spoken, and nonverbal messages—are called information. Whenever something not perfectly predictable happens to a person, he is said to have been presented with information. The storage of information in memory, the retrieval of information from memory, and the execution of a movement in response to information are called information processing.

Limitations of Information Processing

While people have a remarkable capacity for the storage and retrieval of information and for movement control, particularly fine movements of the hands and fingers, they do have limitations. Two kinds of limitations on human performance, identified by Posner and Keele (1970b), are limitations of time and limitations of space.

Limitations of Time

Storage of information in memory involves limitations of time in two different ways. First, the length of time that stored information persists is limited.[1] In fact, the initial products of memory, here called short-term sensory storage, may persist for only a second or so. Slightly more persistent storage, called short-term memory, may persist for only ten to twenty seconds. Long-term memory is much more persistent. The second limitation of time is the amount of time required for information to be transformed into more persistent and abstract representations of events in memory. Chapters 2 and 3 describe the modes of representation in memory and their limitations.

Retrieval of information from memory also requires time. The minimum time that elapses from the presentation of a signal to the initiation of a movement in response to the signal is about one-sixth of a second for humans. Any complication, such as an increase in the number of possible signals and responses, poor discriminability of signals, or a poor relationship between signals and their corresponding responses, increases retrieval time for information regarding the appropriate response. These and other variables affecting the retrieval process are discussed in chapter 5.

Finally, movements also take time. A movement that is controlled by the individual, such as reaching for and grasping an object, takes a minimum of one-tenth of a second. Most movements take more time. Factors affecting the performance of controlled movements are discussed in chapter 6.

Limitations of Space

Limitations of space also influence information processing. If some task cannot be performed simultaneously with another processing task, then some aspect of both the tasks is said to take space. For tasks that involve no such interference it may be concluded that either one or both tasks require no space.

It is often assumed that processes that take time also demand space. This is not necessarily true. People can simultaneously walk and talk, and neither activity interferes notably with the other. Hence, the processes involved in one or both of the tasks must require no space. Conversing and typing, in contrast, appear to interfere strongly with each other, despite the fact that the

[1]Psychologists often make a distinction between availability and accessibility of stored information: material may be stored and available but for some reason no longer accessible. In this book, stored information, as used here, means accessible information.

two tasks use completely different sensory and motor systems. The interference must arise, therefore, at a more central level. Some process involved in conversing and some process involved in typing each take space, so that both processes cannot occur simultaneously without interference. Chapters 3, 5, and 6 include discussions of the space requirements of storage, retrieval, and movement control.

Attention

The study of limitations of space also offers an approach to the old and intriguing problem of the nature of attention. One use of the term *attention* implies that when a person is attending to one thing, he cannot simultaneously attend to something else. Typing is said to require attention because one cannot simultaneously type and participate in conversation. Walking is said to require very little attention because other tasks performed simultaneously, such as thinking, interfere very little with walking. This usage of the term *attention* is virtually the same as our definition of limitations of space, and measures of interference between tasks—that is, their space requirements—is the primary indicator of attention used in this book.

Very early in the history of psychological research, some investigators suggested that attention might be understood in terms of task interference. Binet reported in 1890 that the task of mental addition interfered with the task of squeezing a rubber ball at a regular rate for a predetermined number of times. However, in cases where the number of repetitive movements and the movement accuracy did not need to be monitored, Binet found that there was no interference from a task such as reading. A few years later, Welch (1898) showed that the maintenance of a strong hand grip deteriorated during the performance of various mental tasks such as arithmetic tasks. At about the same time as these early reports of interference between tasks, Bliss (1892) reported that the regularity of tapping was actually facilitated by mental addition. However, a later and more thorough study by Boder (1935) found no such improvement of a repetitive task while the subject was distracted. No general conclusions emerged from these early exploratory efforts to understand attention, but some interesting questions were raised, and a technique for studying attention was developed. To study attention, the investigator observes the performance of two tasks first performed separately and then performed simultaneously and compares the performances in the two situations. Task performances that deteriorate under simultaneous conditions are said to demand attention.

For many years, little work was done on attention, but since the mid-1950s there has been a resurgence of research interest in the problem. Aspects of attention specific to storage, retrieval, and movement control are discussed in chapters 3, 5, and 6, and a general theory of attention is developed in chapter 7.

Applications

The study of human information processing is relatively recent. Research in the field was greatly stimulated by the development of a formal system of information measurement by Shannon and Weaver in 1949 and by attempts made during World War II to design machines that would take into account limitations of human performance. Because the field is new, there have been few practical applications as yet. Some implications for training of skills are explored in chapter 6, and more general implications are suggested in chapter 8. The reader may also wish to consider the possible practical applications of the principles discussed in this book.

 Chapter 2

REPRESENTATION IN MEMORY

One of the basic questions about memory is whether memory is a unitary phenomenon or a system of different storage mechanisms. There are two reasons for raising this question. In the first place, information received from the environment can come through different sensory systems—the visual, auditory, kinesthetic and tactual, gustatory, and olfactory systems, and the sense of balance. The same information can be presented in very different ways—the same word can be presented visibly, audibly, and even tangibly, as in Braille. Even within a single sensory system, a word can be presented differently—as a spoken word or in Morse code. Is the representation in memory the same regardless of the modality and form through which the information is presented, or does the representation retain characteristics peculiar to the mode of input? Is information presented through one modality bound to that form of representation, or is transformation from one form to another possible?

A second reason for raising questions about the structure of memory is the time factor. Stored information can be retrieved less than a second after the original exposure, seconds later, or at much later times. Subjectively, people often feel that the nature of the stored information is different at these different times. It may be that immediately upon experiencing some input, there is a sensation peculiar to the mode of presentation, a sensory image, so to speak. But the input may then be transformed. Even though words are presented visually, a person may say them to himself.

This chapter, therefore, analyzes the nature of representation in memory as deduced from experimental evidence. Evidence is reported which shows that there are very short-lasting representations of material specific to the modality of input, called short-term sensory storage. Either while the original material is still present or while it is in short-term sensory storage, it may be recoded to another form, called short-term memory. A third, more lasting product is called long-term memory.

Short-Term Sensory Storage

It has long been known that, following a very short exposure to a list of items, people can recall only about five to eight items. They think that they can remember more, but by the time they recall a half-dozen items or so, they have forgotten the others. It is as though the sensory impression of a stimulus persisted for a brief time after the stimulus was gone and then faded out, leaving a memory residue different from that initially present. This phenomenon suggests two questions. Is more material briefly stored than can be recalled? Is such storage modality-specific?

Short-Term Visual Storage

Sperling (1960) introduced a technique demonstrating that more items are indeed available immediately after visual stimulus presentation than can be recalled. He showed subjects three lines, each having four letters, for a total duration of only fifty milliseconds. When subjects were asked to recall all the letters that they could, an average of only four or five were recalled. To determine whether more items were available than could be recalled, Sperling devised a partial-report technique. Immediately after the visual stimulus presentation, a high, medium or low frequency tone was presented to indicate which of the three lines of letters should be reported. Subjects did not know in advance which tone would be presented. If, for any line indicated, subjects could recall on the average three of the four letters, it could be deduced that at least three-quarters of the total twelve items—that is nine items—were potentially available. Using this method, Sperling inferred that about ten of the twelve items were available for recall immediately after presentation. It can be concluded that there is a very brief memory, at least for visually presented materials, but that by the time some items are recalled, the others have been forgotten.

How long does such storage persist? Mackworth (1963) determined the length of time digits are reported following a brief exposure of an array of digits. She found that digits were reported with at least 50 percent accuracy for as long as one to two seconds. In that time, about four or five digits were reported. Digits recalled after longer intervals showed greater error. Using the 50 percent criterion, Mackworth claims that visual storage persists approximately one to two seconds.

Mackworth's estimate agrees well with one by Averbach and Sperling (1961), who used a modification of the partial-report technique described above. They presented an array of eighteen letters followed by an auditory signal indicating the single letter to be recalled. The percentage of times that the single letter was recognized yielded an estimate of the total number of letters that were available. When the indicator immediately followed the array of letters, nearly all items were estimated to be available. But when the indicator was delayed, the number of items available declined. Figure 1 shows that the rate of decline depended on lighting conditions. Under normal lighting conditions, the number of available items declined and levelled out by one-half second. This estimate of time in visual storage agrees with Mackworth's estimate. But when it was dark before and after letter exposure, storage persisted in a usable form for about five seconds.

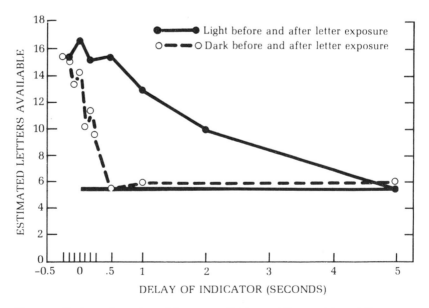

Figure 1. Estimated number of letters available at different delays following a brief exposure of 18 letters. The top two curves are based on the partial report technique. The solid line at the bottom is based on complete report. (Revised from Averbach and Sperling, 1961)

By what criteria can this brief storage be called visual? There are four lines of evidence. First, a subsequent visual presentation, such as a bright light, a checkerboard pattern, or a mixture of lines, immediately following list presentation, reduces the items available for recall (see Averbach 1963, Sperling 1963). Subsequent auditory presentations, however, do not interfere; the tone Sperling (1960) used to cue the line to be reported did not interfere. Second, if the lighting is brighter during exposure of items (Keele and Chase 1967), or if it is dark before and after exposure (see Fig. 1), the storage persists longer, sometimes as long as five seconds. Third, when reporting is slightly delayed, many of the errors are visual confusions (Keele and Chase 1967); that is, the erroneously reported item is visually similar to a presented letter (for example, an 0 for a Q). It is as though the image of the items had faded, making visual confusions more likely. Finally, Eriksen and Collins (1968), in an ingenious study, presented two successive patterns of dots. The dots in each presentation were scattered and unfamiliar, but when the two patterns were superimposed, they formed three letters. The letters could be identified with fair accuracy even when a hundred milliseconds separated the two exposures, implying that the first exposure was preserved in a visual memory. These four sources of evidence—visual masking, brightness factors, visual confusions, and merging of successive patterns—all indicate that the brief storage is indeed visual in nature.

Readout from Visual Storage

A further question concerning visual storage is of interest. When items are visually presented and a report of the items is made, the information derived from visual stimulation must contact information previously stored in memory. If such contact does not occur, the subject will be unable to report the name of what he saw, since names are learned and not intrinsic to the stimulus. Thus, the visual patterns K and WORK must contact memory in order to be translated and reported as the letter k or the word work. This translation of visual material to a form suitable for report has been called readout from sensory storage.

Reicher (1969) addressed himself to the question of whether letters are read out one at a time or simultaneously. He presented in a very brief flash either a single letter such as K, two unrelated letters such as WK, or a four-letter word such as WORK. Following this brief presentation, a field of scrambled parts of letters was presented to terminate visual storage. The effect of the scrambled presentation was to limit the time available for reading out the information from visual store. Subjects were then tested for recognition of a particular letter by being shown, for example, a K and a D and asked to choose which had occurred in the flash. K would be the correct choice in the example given, whether it had occurred alone, in a pair of letters, or in a word. Note that, although only a single letter of the four-letter word need be recognized, either of the possible choices would form a word with the other three letters.

As might be expected, subjects were considerably poorer in recognizing one of two letters than in recognizing the single letter from a one-letter presentation. In the limited time available for readout, one letter was more likely to have been seen than two. Interestingly, though, Reicher found recognition of a letter embedded in a word to be even better than in the single-letter condition. A K was more likely to be chosen if it had been part of a word than if it had occurred alone.

Why is it easier to recall a letter embedded in a word? If the four letters in a word were read out of visual storage one at a time and then assembled into a word, it should take about four times as long to recognize a letter embedded in a word as a single letter. One interpretation is that the visual information from the several letters all simultaneously contact representations stored in memory and are simultaneously translated, yielding a single word-meaning in memory. If two unrelated letters are shown, both presumably contact their separate representatives in memory at the same time, but two units of meaning are activated rather than one, and it is less likely that either can be reported before visual storage is terminated. This interpretation assumes that the names of items in memory remain activated only as long as visual storage persists.

Short-Term Sensory Storage in Other Modalities

Do modalities other than vision, such as auditory, tactual and kinesthetic systems, also exhibit sensory storage? To attack this problem, a direct analogue of Sperling's technique for studying visual storage was used by Bliss, Crane, Mansfield, and Townsend (1966) to study tactual sensory storage. Air jets were positioned under the three interjoint spaces on each of the eight fingers. Up to 12 of the 24 positions were then simultaneously stimulated with a brief hundred-millisecond pulse of air. When subjects attempted to report all the positions stimulated, only about 3.5 positions could be correctly reported. When, however, a signal following the air jets indicated that only the tips of the fingers, the middle positions, or the interjoint positions closest to the palm were to be reported, about 5.2 positions were available in memory immediately after stimulation. The slight superiority of the partial-report technique decayed in about one or two seconds. Thus, tactual storage, like visual storage, is very brief in duration.

An interesting sidelight emerged when Bliss studied a blind person in addition to the normally sighted subjects. The blind subject showed no unusual tactual storage. Although this single piece of evidence is certainly not conclusive, it suggests that sensory storage cannot be improved to any large degree by heavy reliance on that system.

Quite a different technique was developed by Eriksen and Johnson (1964) to study the auditory system. Subjects sat in chairs reading novels that held their interest. At various times, a low-intensity tone occurred that was difficult to detect while reading. A lamp was turned off between 0 and 10.5 seconds after the tone occurred. At that time, the subject was asked to report whether the tone had occurred within the last 15 seconds. To keep the subject honest, the light was sometimes turned off when no tone had been presented.

The results of the experiment showed that the percentage of times the tone was correctly detected declined steadily as the delay between tone and light was lengthened to 10.5 seconds. Short-term acoustic storage appears to persist as long as ten seconds, somewhat longer than visual and tactual storage. However, if the person is not alerted to the presence of the stimulus within that period, there is a chance that it will go undetected.

The acoustic storage time found by Eriksen and Johnson is quite similar to storage time inferred from an experiment by Wickelgren (1966). Wickelgren found that the ability to tell whether or not two successive tones were the same frequency declined as the separation between the tones increased to eight seconds.

Sounds more complex than tones may deteriorate faster than ten seconds. There is some evidence that numbers and letters presented through the auditory mode are available from short-term acoustic storage in usable form for only two to three seconds (see Crowder and Morton 1969). This faster deterioration may be due not to a faster loss from acoustic storage but to the fact that a higher quality image is needed to identify a letter than a tone. Still, the storage time is longer than short-term visual storage.

Another sensory system that has been studied is the kinesthetic system, which provides information on felt position and movement of the limbs. Posner and Konick (1966) asked subjects to move a lever until it was stopped by a peg. Then, at various retention intervals, the subjects attempted to reproduce the length of movement with another lever. The accuracy of reproduction declined over an approximately twenty-second retention interval. Later work by Williams, Beaver, Spence, and Rundell (1969) indicated that such memory was indeed kinesthetic. Extraneous movements interpolated during the retention interval interfered with retention, but retention was unaffected by the recording, adding, or classifying of numbers during the retention period. Other studies of kinesthetic memory (Keele and Ells 1972, Montgomery 1971) found little spontaneous forgetting, however, and instead forgetting occurred only when distracting mental tasks were interpolated in the retention period. These conflicting results appear attributable to the great complexity of the kinesthetic system, which involves a number of different sensory components. Laabs (1971) found that those kinesthetic cues that help people locate positions in space do not show spontaneous forgetting, while those cues underlying memory for distance do show spontaneous loss, suggesting different sensory stores. But the storage characteristics of different kinesthetic cues are still not known.

Kinesthetic memory is of direct interest to people interested in motor skills. In addition, some recent theorists have suggested that the motor system is important in perception and memory. There is evidence that short-term memory for verbal materials involves the motor system. Also, the storage time of short-term verbal memory is similar to that of kinesthetic memory.

Recoding in Memory

There is evidence supporting the view that information from the environment persists in a sensory store for about one second for vision and up to perhaps twenty seconds for kinesthesis. What is the nature of representation once these brief stores decay? Is the information recoded into some form quite different from the original input to the memory system?

Visual-to-Auditory Recoding

One way of assessing the nature of representation is to analyze errors in recall. Such errors should exhibit different characteristics depending on the form of memory. When more letters are briefly presented than can be reported correctly, some errors are due to visual confusions. Suppose only a few letters are exposed long enough to allow the letters to be read out from sensory storage. What errors occur then?

Conrad (1964) selected two sets of letters that were similar within a set but not between sets. One set was the letters B, C, P, T, and V, all of which end with an ē sound. The other set was F, M, N, S, and X, which all start with an ĕ sound. From these two sets, lists of six letters were constructed. Each letter in a list was visually presented for 0.75 seconds, which is adequate time for reading, and then subjects were immediately asked to recall the list. For simplicity, Conrad analyzed only those cases in which exactly one letter of the six was incorrectly recalled. He found that the errors were usually auditory confusions even though the letters had been visually presented. For instance, if the letter P had been presented and a recall error was made, the letter V would more probably be substituted than the letter F, even though F is visually more similar to P.

Given time for reading, memory for letters usually appears to be transformed from a visual to an auditory code. The form that is stored no longer conforms to the mode of input. One implication of such a transformation is that much of the original input may not be recoverable. If only the auditory sound is retained, then the knowledge of whether A or a had been presented visually will have been lost. Typically, the recoded memory is more abstract than the original sensory storage.

A further experiment by Conrad and Rush (1965) raises, but does not fully answer, another interesting question about the form of memory. Five-letter lists from the same sets mentioned earlier were visually presented to deaf children. These subjects showed no evidence of auditory confusions. More interesting, the errors were not visually similar to the correct letter either.

How are letters represented in the memories of deaf people? One possibility is that, if the deaf person knows sign language, the errors in memory are sign language confusions. Many years ago Watson (1924) suggested that thinking involved the motor system. Deaf persons observed in the process of thinking often move their fingers. Conrad and Rush (as reported in Conrad 1970) also observed some of their subjects using sign language while memorizing. More recently, Locke and Locke (1971) found convincing evidence that some deaf people store visually presented letters in a motor system. Deaf persons who spoke poorly but knew sign language often substituted in recall a letter that had similar finger spelling for the correct letter. Hearing subjects did not show the same type of confusion.

Some deaf people speak quite well even though they may have

become deaf prior to learning language. Both Conrad (1970) and Locke and Locke (1971) showed that deaf subjects who spoke well showed auditory confusions in recall of letters. These findings suggest that the memory code was of a motor type related to speech production rather than a sensory code.

Articulatory versus Acoustic Storage

The question raised about recoding with deaf subjects can also be raised for normal hearing subjects. Is the recoded memory of visually presented information of a sensory type or of a motor type? The auditory system is actually composed of two anatomically distinct parts—a sensory system for receiving sounds, which may be called an acoustic system, and a motor system for producing sounds, the articulatory system. Earlier, brief storage for material presented through the auditory mode was referred to as short-term *acoustic* storage because it seems more sensory than motor in character. It is possible, however, that an auditory signal, such as a spoken letter, can be transformed into an articulatory code. In other words, it is possible that information that has been read out from short-term sensory storage is recoded in another sensory store—in this case an acoustic store—or it may be recoded in a motor store—articulatory.

At present, there is no way of knowing directly which is the case, but there is some indirect evidence bearing on the question. Hintzman (1965) observed that when people memorize visually presented letters during exposure to white noise, they often say the letters out loud. The implication is that the articulation process is usually used in memorizing, and during exposure to white noise, people fail to suppress the overt act of articulating. Murray (1968) found that when subjects were forced to articulate an irrelevant word while letters were being visually presented for storage, recall of the letters no longer showed auditory confusions. This again suggests that auditory coding is of an articulatory rather than an acoustic form. If something interferes with articulation of the letters to be stored, articulatory coding disappears, and another form of representation, perhaps visual, takes its place.

A quite different approach to the articulatory-acoustic issue was presented by Crowder and Morton (1969). A list of digits to be recalled was presented through the auditory mode. An additional 0 was spoken as a suffix to the list but was not to be recalled. A control list had no such suffix. The additional digit interfered with recall of the last few items in the experimental list. A subsequent auditory event, therefore, seems to interfere with the retention of auditory events that slightly precede it. Interference extends to items that occur two or three seconds earlier, suggesting that short-term acoustic storage for complex auditory materials is usable for a shorter time than it is for tones.

If the recoding of visually presented items into an auditory mode were also acoustic rather than articulatory, then one might expect that a subsequent auditory suffix would cause interference. But interference of the sort found with auditory list presentation does not occur with visual list presentation. This suggests that the recoded product is not an acoustic image, or at least it is not an image that other auditory events can interfere with. The implication instead is that the auditory storage resulting from visual input is of an articulatory nature.

One caution should be noted. The notion of articulatory coding does not imply that the vocal apparatus necessarily moves, although Hintzman observed that subjects moved their lips during exposure to white noise. The vocal apparatus is controlled by neural activity in the brain. It is entirely possible that some aspect of that neural activity can occur without actual stimulation of the muscles involved.

There is evidence that verbal material presented through the auditory mode is also translated to an articulatory form rather than remaining in some form of acoustic storage. Indeed it is argued by some (such as Liberman, Cooper, Shankweiler and Studdert-Kennedy, 1967) that when verbal material is perceived through the auditory mode, it is perceived in terms of the articulatory mechanism that would yield the sound. This is the motor theory of speech perception. Quite different acoustic patterns may be produced by similar articulatory patterns. For example, the b in bat and in but have different acoustic patterns, as measured by a sound spectrogram. When people listen to the sounds, however, they sound the same, presumably because they arise from the same articulatory mechanism.

The motor system, or central components of that system, do appear to play a role in thinking—at least in perceiving and memorizing verbal information. When verbal material is presented, it is retained briefly in a sensory storage system peculiar to the input modality, whether visual or auditory. But recoding quickly follows, and the form of representation is then motor. For hearing people, the typical motor representation is articulatory. For the deaf, it may be either articulatory or sign language.

Auditory-to-Visual Recoding

Evidence has been reviewed which suggests that visual and auditory presentations may be recoded in memory in an articulatory form. It may be that articulatory coding is particularly useful for dealing with verbal materials. For other information, however, it may be that a visual code is more useful. Some problems, such as furniture rearrangement, might be more easily solved in a visual mode. The question of whether transformation can also occur from an auditory input to a visual code may seem to be absurd. It seems obvious that people can visually represent information in memory. However, some people claim to have very weak visual images, if any at all, and there is little agreement as to what constitutes an image. Certainly few visual images retain as much detail as does a photograph. Most important, however, what people say about their visual images reveals little about important properties of imagery. A study by Brooks (1967) not only presented some interesting evidence about imagery, but also showed that visual imagery involves some of the same mechanisms as does visual perception.

Brooks thought that translating information into a visual image would be more difficult when the input came through the visual system (since that system would already be occupied with visual processing) than when input came through the auditory system. Subjects in Brooks's study either listened to or simultaneously read and listened to a series of sentences such as, "In the next square to the *right* put a 2; in the next square *up* put a 3; in the next square to the *right* put a 4," and so on up to the number 8, while they were imagining a 4 × 4 matrix. An example of what a person might store is shown in figure 2. After the presenta-

SPATIAL MATERIAL

In the starting square put a 1.
In the next square to the **right** put a 2.
In the next square **up** put a 3.
In the next square to the **right** put a 4.
In the next square **down** put a 5.
In the next square **down** put a 6.
In the next square to the **left** put a 7.
In the next square **down** put an 8.

NONSENSE MATERIAL

In the starting square put a 1.
In the next square to the **quick** put a 2.
In the next square to the **good** put a 3.
In the next square to the **quick** put a 4.
In the next square to the **bad** put a 5.
In the next square to the **bad** put a 6.
In the next square to the **slow** put a 7.
In the next square to the **bad** put an 8.

		3	4
1	2	5	
		7	6
		8	

Figure 2. Examples of sentences read or listened to, and an illustration of how spatial material can be mentally recorded to a visual form. (From Brooks, 1967)

tion of the sentences, the subjects tried to recall which word (*right, left, up, down*) was paired with which number. The subjects averaged 2.8 errors in recall when they had read and listened to the sentences but only 1.2 errors when they had only listened to the sentences.

It is tempting to conclude that visualization competes more with other uses of the visual system, such as reading, than it does with other systems, such as the auditory system. An alternate explanation, however, is that reading merely results in poorer recall than does listening, and that the results have nothing to do with visualization. To control for this possibility, Brooks performed a similar experiment but with nonspatial words— *quick, slow, good,* and *bad.* Reading and listening together resulted in an average of 1.3 recall errors, while listening alone resulted in 2.3 errors, the contrary of the earlier experiment. Since in the control experiment reading and listening proved better than simply listening, there is nothing about reading inherently causing poorer recall.

The results appear to be explainable only by assuming that: (1) sentences denoting spatial direction can be recoded into visual images (or more properly spatial images; Brooks also demonstrated conflict between imaging and movements to positions in space); and (2) visualization uses some of the same processes as does seeing. Subsequent work by Brooks (1968) showed that people are not only able to visualize images, but such visualization can be manipulated—for example, the image can be rotated. Such manipulative abilities appear to be useful not just for memorizing but also for solving some types of problems. For the interested reader, further evidence of auditory-to-visual recoding has been presented by Posner, Boies, Eichelman, and Taylor (1969).

Coding Flexibility

The evidence reviewed indicates that once information is perceived a great deal of flexibility exists for the form of recoding. Verbal materials often are coded in an articulatory form, even when presentation is visual. Spatial material may be visually coded, even when presentation is auditory. Although the new code may be in a different mode than the presentation mode, evidence is accumulating that a transformation in mode is not necessary. It was already mentioned that auditory input may be retained in a basically auditory mode, although the exact representation appears transformed from a sensory-acoustic storage to a motor-articulatory storage. Also some evidence indicates that in some circumstances visually presented letters may be maintained in a visual code. For example, Warrington and Shallice (1972) studied a brain damaged patient that has a specific deficit for short-term recall of auditorily presented letters. Such a deficit does not occur in this patient for visually presented letters. Furthermore, recall errors following visually presented letters did not exhibit auditory confusions as Conrad found for normal subjects. Instead visual confusions occurred, suggesting a recoding from sensory visual storage to a more persistent visual store.

Normal people also appear able to code letters visually as well as auditorily. Parks, Kroll, Salzberg, and Parkinson (1972) visually presented a single letter for recognition eight seconds later. During the retention interval the auditory system was loaded by presenting a succession of spoken letters to be repeated by the subjects. In view of the high auditory load it would be to the subject's advantage were he able to maintain the visual letter in a visual code. In fact the subjects did appear to maintain a visual code, since they were faster at recognizing a letter that had the same shape as earlier (e.g., both capital Bs) than a letter that had the same name but had changed in shape (e.g., a b followed eight seconds later by a B). Had the visual letter been coded only in auditory form, no difference in recognition time would have been expected.

Recoded memory may or may not differ in form from the original input; memory representation does not depend solely on the form of input but also on the demands of the task. Nevertheless, even when the basic modality of input is maintained, the recoded form of memory may differ in another way. Some evidence suggests a motor based representation for recoded memory rather than a sensory based representation, although data is not complete for all possible transforms.

Short-Term Memory (STM) and Long-Term Memory (LTM)

We have seen that the first stage of memory, short-term sensory storage, is brief in duration and is replaced by another code. How long does this second stage persist? Although some studies are beginning to differentiate the persistence time of recoded visual memory from that of recoded auditory memory, this distinction will not be pursued here. We may also ask whether the recoded product is a final stage of memory or whether a further stage of memory must be postulated.

If only a few items such as letters are presented, the items can be remembered for essentially unlimited amounts of time by rehearsing. But when rehearsal is prevented, memory for even a few items is brief indeed. In a now classic study by Peterson and Peterson (1959) a three-consonant list (such as XJQ) was spelled out and then immediately followed by a three-digit number. To prevent rehearsal, subjects counted backwards by threes from the number given at the rate of one count per second until a signal to recall the letters was given either three, six, nine, twelve, fifteen, or eighteen seconds later. Following recall, another three-letter list was presented, and so on. The proportion of times that a three-letter sequence was correctly recalled at the successive time intervals was 0.8, 0.6, 0.3, 0.2, 0.1, and finally slightly less than 0.1 at the eighteen-second interval. After only eighteen seconds, less than one-tenth of the sequences could be remembered correctly.

Murdock (1961) wondered whether the number of letters per se was critical for recall or whether the number of meaningful units was critical. As shown in figure 3, essentially the same retention loss over time is exhibited for three words as for three unrelated letters. One word shows much less loss even though it involves several letters.

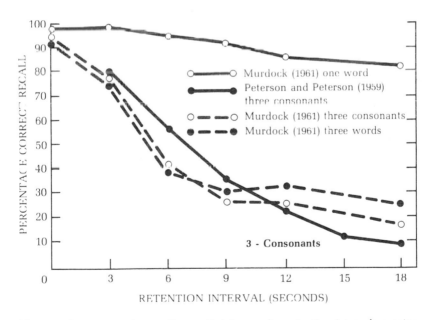

Figure 3. Percentage of correctly recalled items after retention intervals ranging from 0 to 18 seconds. The items to be recalled were either single words, 3 words, or 3 letters. (From Melton, 1963)

Murdock's experiment should be compared with Reicher's study (1969) on readout from visual storage discussed earlier. Both suggest that the primary limitation in dealing with information from the environment is the number of units activated in memory and not the number of letters in the units. People rehearse words, not letters from words.

The very rapid forgetting when rehearsal is prevented has suggested to some theorists (such as Brown 1958) that the second state of memory is not the final state. This second state has come to be called short-term memory (STM) to distinguish it from long-term memory (LTM). Because most forgetting when rehearsal is prevented occurs in ten to twenty seconds, that is the usual assumed duration of STM. Any residual recall after that period is thought to be due to the proportion of items that have entered LTM. Some versions of the theory (such as that of Waugh and Norman 1965) have suggested that it is not time elapsed per se that causes STM loss but the interpolation of other items that compete for limited space in STM. Other investigators (such as Melton 1963, Underwood and Keppel 1963) have suggested that STM and LTM are really the same process, differing only in strength due to degree of practice. With one presentation and limited rehearsal, forgetting is evident in just a few seconds. With repeated practice, memory is the same but more resistant to forgetting, and consequently it shows less loss over a short period of time.

Three lines of evidence suggest that STM and LTM are different processes: (1) clinical evidence from brain injury cases, (2) evidence of different effects of spacing of practice on retention at long and short time intervals, and (3) evidence that the nature of representation in memory is different at long and short retention intervals. (In the next chapter, a fourth line of evidence is developed—amount of information has different effects on immediate recall and longer term learning.)

Effects of Brain Injury on Memory

One treatment for very severe cases of epilepsy is to remove portions of the brain from which the seizures emanate. Although this sounds like a drastic measure, in most cases there is little or only temporary impairment of mental functioning. In 1953, H. M. had a bilateral removal of much of the hippocampus and some surrounding areas. Several people had previously undergone unilateral removal of the hippocampus with relatively minor mental impairment.

Following surgery, H. M.'s IQ showed little change, but there was a severe impairment of memory (Milner, Corkin, and Teuber 1968). Although he could remember quite well events that had occurred at least two years previous to the operation, he was with rare exceptions unable to recall events that occurred subsequent to the operation. He could not, for example, recognize people he had met the day before. Verbal learning experiments, which required that he learn material and recall it at a much later time, indicated little or no retention. In contrast to his inability to store information for long retention intervals, H. M. apparently had a normal STM. Wickelgren (1968) presented to him a list of three-digit numbers. Then another three-digit number was presented, and H. M. was asked to recall whether that number had appeared in the preceding list. He recognized items quite well at very short delays following presentation, but by ten seconds he had largely forgotten them. These results are similar to those found with normal subjects; when rehearsal is prevented, items which were recently presented are preserved in STM, but items presented earlier are usually forgotten. However, if the same list were repeated over and over, normal subjects would eventually remember the entire list, and H. M. would not. The conclusion drawn from studying H. M. is that, for verbal materials, STM is different from LTM.

Although H. M. was unable to retain verbal materials from one day to the next, there was improvement on some motor tasks on successive days of practice (Corkin 1968). The detailed manner in which improvement occurred differed from normals though. Apparently somewhat different processes are involved in storage of verbal materials in LTM and the development of motor skills.

Talland (1967) has reported that chronic alcoholics suffering from Korsakoff's syndrome may also show an impairment of the ability to store information in LTM, again supporting the distinction between STM and LTM.

Recently, Shallice and Warrington (1970) described a patient, K. F., whose impairment was the opposite of H. M.'s. Since K. F. had suffered brain damage in an accident, the locus of damage was not as well specified as in the case of H. M. K. F. had an essentially normal recall at long retention intervals, but recall at short intervals was severely impaired. Shallice and Warrington repeated the Peterson and Peterson paradigm with K. F. Three three-letter words were presented through the auditory mode, and then K. F. counted forward by ones as rapidly as possible for five, ten, or fifteen seconds before recall. For K. F., recall was essentially the same at all intervals, with no improvement at the shortest interval. It is as though at the time of presentation the item was stored in LTM with a certain probability of recall, but there was no simultaneous storage in STM with its subsequent decay.

In a later study of K. F., Warrington and Shallice (1972) varied the number of letters to be held in STM and the modality through which the letters were presented. The results are shown in figure 4. With only one or two input items through the auditory mode, there was some residual STM: the auditory STM impairment is not complete. Visually projected items, however, were retained normally. Thus, we may conclude not only that STM is different than LTM, but that STM may be either visual or auditory in nature.

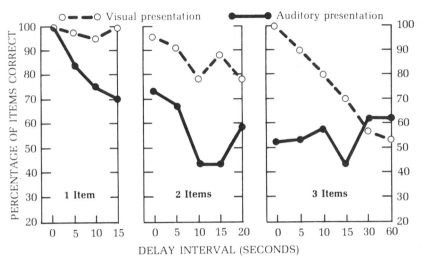

Figure 4. Percentage of letters recalled by K. F. at different retention intervals. (From Warrington and Shallice. 1972)

The Spacing Effect

If STM is a different process from LTM, then one might expect to find conditions that facilitate recall at intervals less than about ten seconds but affect recall at longer intervals differently. One such case is the spacing effect discovered by Peterson, Hillner, and Saltzman (1962). They presented to subjects a list of word-number pairs. Each pair was presented twice to enable the subjects to learn it. In the massed condition, the two presentations of a pair were made contiguously. In the spaced condition, eight seconds intervened between the two presentations. With eight seconds' spacing, the interval between presentations was filled with other pairs to prevent rehearsal. Following the second presentation of the pair, the word was presented alone either two, four, eight, or sixteen seconds later and at that time the subjects attempted to recall the number that had been paired with the word. The retention interval between the second learning trial and the recall test was also filled with other pairs to prevent rehearsal. Thus, there were two learning trials, either spaced or massed, and then a retention test at different times following the second learning trial.

The percentages of correct recall in the various conditions are shown in figure 5. It can be seen that recall at longer retention intervals is best when the two learning trials were spaced eight seconds apart. Recall at the shorter intervals was just the opposite; better recall occurred when the two learning trials were presented contiguously. These results give additional support to the notion that STM is different from LTM. Contiguous repetition of an item to be recalled apparently strengthens the representation in STM. However, spacing of practice is better for storing information in LTM.

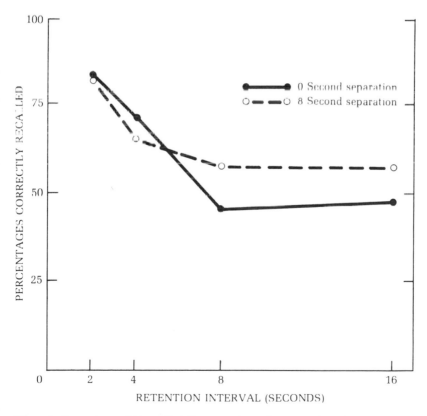

Figure 5. Percentage of times that the correct number was given in response to a stimulus word at varying retention intervals after the last learning trial. In one condition the two learning trials were separated by eight seconds; in the other condition the learning trials had no separation. (Data from Peterson, Hillner, and Saltzman, 1962)

Representation in LTM

Finally, if STM is different from LTM, it is possible that the nature of representation is different in the two systems. It has been argued that verbal materials are normally recoded into an auditory form for STM. A number of quite ingenious experiments have suggested that LTM, in contrast, stores meaning.

If LTM stores meaning, then it might be expected that errors would tend to be semantic in form when recall is delayed beyond the assumed duration of STM, about ten seconds. *Bucket* might be erroneously recalled or recognized when *pail* was presented. Evidence for semantic confusions after long retention intervals has been presented by Underwood (1965), Anisfeld and Knapp (1968), and Grossman and Eagle (1970).

A different approach used by Kolers (1966) also supports the idea that meaning rather than the sound of words is stored in LTM. When bilingual subjects were to recall a long list of words, one English and one French presentation of words having the same meaning, such as *dog* and *chien*, resulted in recall as good as when there were two presentations of the word in the same language. Recently, Kintsch (1970) extended Koler's technique and found that bilinguals often do not remember the language in which a word was presented.

It may be argued, however, that none of these experiments tested whether auditory coding might also exist at long retention intervals. A study by Kintsch and Buschke (1969) deals with this question. It has been known for some time that learning items in a specified order is more difficult when the items are similar to each other than when they are dissimilar. Kintsch and Buschke reasoned, therefore, that if STM involves auditory coding and LTM does not, and if there are words in the same list that sound alike, such as *pair* and *pear*, then there should be interference with recall of recently presented items but not with recall of items presented about ten or more seconds earlier. On the other hand, lists containing synonyms, such as *bucket* and *pail*, should not adversely affect recall of recent items but should adversely affect recall of items presented earlier.

To test these predictions, lists of sixteen words were constructed. In one experiment, there was one list of sixteen unrelated words and another list of eight pairs of synonyms. A word was presented every two seconds. Immediately following the presentation, one word was presented and the subjects were asked to recall the word that had followed it on the list. The probabilities of correctly recalling words from various positions on the list are shown in figure 6. Items that had been in memory only a short time were recalled well (item 16 was the last presented), but items that had been in memory for several seconds had a low probability of recall, particularly for the synonym list. In the second experiment, homonym pairs were used instead of synonym pairs. The items were visually presented so that homonyms could be distinguished from one another. The results are shown in figure 7. As expected, auditory similarity had the greatest adverse effect on recently presented material.

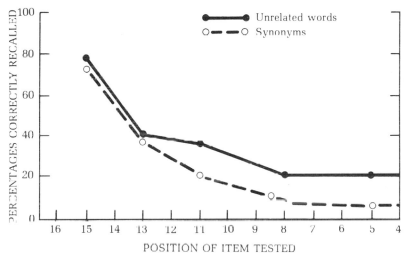

Figure 6. Percentage of correct recall for words presented at different positions on list of synonyms and unrelated words. The 16th item presented has been in memory the least time. (Adapted from Kintsch and Bushke, 1969)

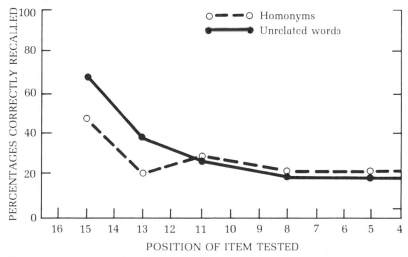

Figure 7. Percentages of correct recall for words presented at different positions on lists of homonyms and unrelated words. (Adapted from Kintsch and Bushke, 1969)

The Kintsch and Buschke study indicates that the dominant mode of representation at long recall intervals is different from that at short intervals and supports the idea that STM and LTM are different processes. It would certainly be in error, however, to conclude that auditory properties are never represented in LTM. While auditory-to-semantic recoding may be a normal course for verbal materials, situations may arise in which auditory cues are useful in recall from LTM. To cite one example, Craik and Levy (1970) visually presented a list of twenty words to be recalled. In one case, the words presented near the middle of the list (positions six through eleven) were similar in sound (such as *pillow*, *fellow*, and *hollow*). In another case, the words were unrelated. Following item presentation, subjects recalled the words in whatever order they could.[1] It might be expected that recall of one word would prompt recall of another word from LTM that sounded the same, and in fact, Craik and Levy did find superior recall of the similar sounding words. This superiority was much reduced when the original learning pace was speeded up. With a fast learning pace, there was less time to incorporate the auditory code in LTM.

Visual LTM

So far, the discussion has dealt primarily with representation of verbal materials in memory. Much of what we remember, however, is not verbal. We see a three-toed sloth. At a later time, we see another three-toed sloth and recognize having seen one before. If we have artistic talent, we can even draw the animal from memory. Recognition and recall of visual forms require that visual information be retained in memory.

There is an old controversy concerning the nature of visual representation in LTM. In 1710, Bishop Berkeley (see Sampson 1897, pp. 165, 148) argued that individual examples of a class of objects are independently represented in memory. ("Whatever hand or eye I imagine, it must have some particular shape or colour. Likewise, the idea of man that I frame to myself must be either of a white, or a black, or a tawny, a straight, or a crooked, a tall, or a low, or a middle-sized man. I cannot by any effort of thought conceive the *abstract* idea.") John Locke, in contrast, argued in 1690 that from members of a category of objects a

---

[1]The method of recall is probably critical. Kintsch and Buschke required that the order of the items presented be retained. While a similar sounding word may prompt the recall of another, it may not facilitate recalling the correct order.

more general representation of the class is abstracted. ("If every particular idea that we take in should have a distinct name, names must be endless. To prevent this, the mind makes the particular ideas, received from particular objects, to become general.") Locke's abstraction might be thought of as an average or as a composite picture. Most interesting, the abstract representation may never actually have been experienced. A milder version of Locke's position is that people retain in memory characteristics of individual examples from a class as well as the abstract representation.

To study the problem of visual abstraction, Posner and Keele (1968) constructed random dot patterns. Such patterns were chosen because they were unfamiliar to subjects and because the degree of similarity between members of a class of dot patterns is easy to control. Prototype patterns were first constructed, and for each prototype several distortions similar to the prototype were constructed by slightly moving the dots to new positions. Since a particular dot sometimes moved one direction in one distorted pattern and another direction in another distortion, the dots in the prototype were approximately in the middle position—i.e., the prototype was the average pattern. An example of three prototypes and four distortions of one of the prototypes is shown in figure 8.

The experiment was conducted in two phases. In the first phase, four distortions of each of three prototypes were selected and presented one at a time to the subject, who then learned to classify them into three categories, with all the distortions from one prototype being put into a single category. After each attempt to classify a pattern, the subject was informed whether he was correct or incorrect. During the initial learning phase, the subjects never saw the prototypes from which the distortions were constructed.

A recognition phase was then conducted in which the subjects were shown several patterns and asked to classify them into the three categories on the basis of previous learning. Some of the patterns were ones previously learned (Old Distortions), some were the Prototypes, which had not previously been seen, and some were New Distortions made from the same prototypes but not previously seen. The Old Distortions were correctly classified 87 percent of the time. Prototypes were classified nearly as well, with 85 percent correct. New Distortions, however, were classified less well, with 73 percent correct.

Since the prototypes, even though not previously seen, were recognized about as well as the Old Distortions, it is argued that the representation of visual patterns in LTM involves abstraction

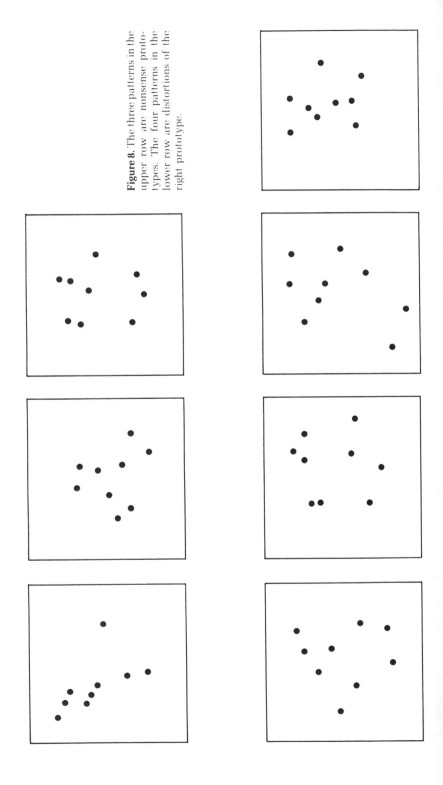

from patterns actually seen. Since the Old Distortions were also recognized better than the New Distortions, it is argued that people retain information about individual patterns as well as about abstractions.

Subsequently, Posner and Keele (1970a) and Strange, Keeney, Kessel, and Jenkins (1970) showed that, over a period of a week, the Prototype suffers little retention loss, while the Old Distortions show substantial loss. It appears that the abstract visual representation is more stable in memory than are individual patterns. As memory for the original exemplars fades out, the recognition of members of the class is presumably mediated by the abstraction.

It can be argued that dot patterns used in these studies are not realistic and that, with more realistic patterns, abstraction may not occur. Reed (1970) showed people line drawings of faces differing in nose length, mouth position, distance between eyes, and forehead height. The subjects learned to classify the faces into two groups. Following classification, they were much better able to identify the prototype of each class than they were able to identify control patterns. Abstraction of information in LTM therefore seems to be common to both verbal and visual materials. Much of the original input is lost, and the result is a product that greatly economizes in processing demands.

Overview of the States of Memory

Memory does not simply reflect whatever impinges on the senses. Stored material undergoes a series of transformations and abstractions. Altogether, three states of memory can be distinguished. Initially, information is retained in short-term sensory storage that exhibits characteristics specific to the mode of presentation. Such storage is quite brief, ranging from approximately one second for visual and tactual inputs to perhaps twenty or so seconds for the kinesthetic system. These durations depend on the conditions of presentation and somewhat arbitrary distinctions as to when the information is no longer useful.

During the time of presentation, or while the material is still in sensory storage, it is transformed from a visual to an articulatory, an auditory to a visual, or an acoustic to an articulatory mode, and perhaps to others. The recoded product, at least for articulatory coding, is itself relatively brief, typically lasting only ten to twenty seconds in the absence of rehearsal. Because it is brief, it is called short-term memory (STM). STM differs from short-term sensory storage in that it lasts longer and appears to be related to the motor system rather than to the sensory system.

A more persistent stage of memory, long-term memory (LTM), appears to be much more abstract. For verbal materials, the meaning of information is usually retained, but the precise form of the information may be lost. Some theorists have suggested that LTM is composed of more than one state—LTM shortly after STM has decayed (ten or twenty seconds after the presentation of information) and LTM an hour, a week, or a year later. Certainly, people can remember much more twenty seconds after information is presented than they can remember a year later. Such forgetting over long periods could be attributed either to loss from a single store or to a change in the storage mechanism. However, evidence that different storage mechanisms are involved at early and late periods is not strong, and further distinctions in LTM must await additional evidence.

Transformations between states of memory take time, and when the information exceeds the amount that can be transformed or rehearsed before decay occurs, some information is lost. Only four or five items can be recalled from a brief visual store before the other items decay. Fortunately, the limitation on readout from visual storage is determined not by the complexity of visual material, but by the number of meaningful units into which the visual information is transformed. Similarly, the rehearsal of material in STM for storage in LTM is limited by the number of meaningful units, not by the complexity in terms of number of letters in a word.

It is important to distinguish between the characteristics of the different states of memory. Sensory store, STM, and LTM cannot be distinguished simply on the basis of the time of recall. LTM, for example, refers to storage that is relatively immune to forgetting, not necessarily to recall after long time intervals. It is entirely possible for information to be stored in both STM and LTM only a few seconds after being presented. However, STM deteriorates rapidly in the absence of rehearsal, and LTM is more persistent. The two forms of representation also differ.

Figures 9 and 10 illustrate a hypothetical set of results from recalling visually presented verbal information. As the delay between the initial presentation and recall is increased up to twenty seconds, there is a rapid decline in the percentage of correctly recalled items. Figure 9 shows the decline in recall. Figure 10 illustrates the hypothetical durations for which information in the different stores is available. For visually presented material, the information is initially available from sensory store. Within a few hundred milliseconds following presentation, the informa-

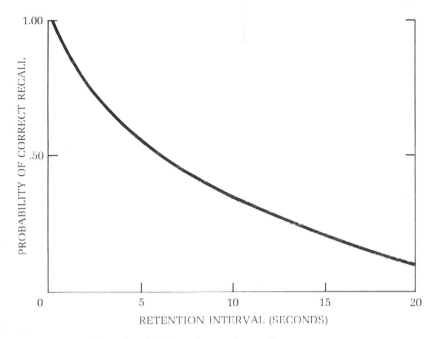

Figure 9. Hypothetical probability of correctly recalling items at various retention intervals.

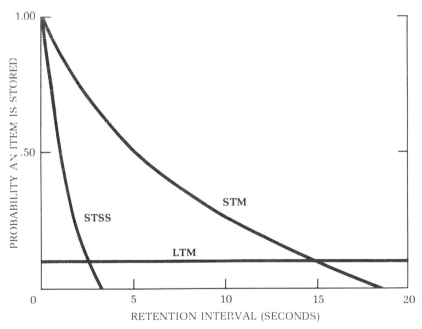

Figure 10. Illustrates hypothetical durations of three storage systems: short-term sensory storage (STSS), short-term memory (STM), and long-term memory (LTM).

tion is recoded into STM, and some proportion of the material enters LTM. Thus, at the shortest intervals, information can conceivably be recalled from any of the three stores. Within two seconds after presentation, sensory storage deteriorates and STM deteriorates slightly, so the probability of recalling the information also decreases slightly. By fifteen seconds, STM is gone, and recall is dependent on the amount of information that has been recoded into LTM.

Thus, although LTM may be available after short intervals, it is best studied after long intervals, when it is uncontaminated by sensory storage and STM. The failure to consider this possible contamination has often caused confusion about the nature of STM and LTM, and the possibility of multiple representation at short intervals has made it difficult to determine the exact course of development of LTM. Some theorists have suggested that LTM, rather than remaining constant from the time of presentation, as shown in figure 10, shows a gradual buildup over the first five or ten seconds following presentation. Some data support the buildup notion, but the evidence is not strong one way or the other.

Functions of the Memory States

Not much is known yet about the function in everyday tasks of the different memory processes. It is obvious that LTM is useful. H. M., who underwent a bilateral removal of the hippocampus, was not able to store new information in LTM. He was severely handicapped—unable to find his way home or recognize people he had just met. Much less obvious are the implications of the loss of sensory storage capacity, STM, or the ability to transform one form of memory to another.

It is possible that short-term visual storage prevents some loss of information during information overload. Much important visual information has a very brief duration. If the organism is processing other information at the time of presentation, the new information may be lost, but short-term visual storage slightly extends the period of time for which information is available. Sperling (1960) has suggested that such a mechanism is useful in reading. The eye periodically makes saccadic movements from one point of focus to another. Short-term visual storage may allow constant readout of the material even during eye movement. It is possible that people with a deficient sensory storage capacity are also deficient in reading skills.

Short-term acoustic storage is more persistent than visual storage. Because of the brevity of short-term visual storage, the first part of sequentially presented information (such as Morse code) might be unavailable when the last part was presented, and because material is read out from sensory storage in meaningful units, the reading of larger units might thus be prevented. Acoustic storage may overcome this problem. In fact Nazzaro and Nazzaro (1970) have shown that temporal patterns much like Morse code are more difficult to learn with visual presentation than with auditory presentation. Acoustic storage may also be necessary for the understanding of spoken material, which extends over time.

Many problems may be easier to solve if the mode of representation is transformed from that of the original presentation. For instance, it may be considerably easier to transform a verbal description of directions to some destination into a visual map. Transformation to a visual code might also be useful in searching for some item in the visual field. Turnbull (1971) has shown that it is easier to find a letter in a long list when the exact form of the letter (whether it is a capital or a small letter) as well as the name is known.

Some other problems might be easier to solve in an auditory or semantic code than in a visual code, so that the rules of language and other symbol systems such as algebra can be applied. It is probably easier to add 2 and 3 using an auditory code than it is to translate the numbers to visual images of apples and then count the apples. In other situations, the transformation from sensory storage to auditory STM is useful merely to take advantage of its longer persistence, as when dialing a telephone number. Although STM is relatively brief itself, it is still useful to prolong slightly, rehearse, manipulate, or match information. People with deficient STM may be deficient in more general thinking abilities.

Conrad (1971) recently studied children of different ages to determine when the ability to recode from visual to auditory representations develops. He showed children pictures of objects that had either similar or dissimilar names (such as cat and hat, or girl and bus). Only children five years old or older on a mental age scale exhibited greater errors when recalling the list with similar names than when recalling the list with dissimilar names. Even though children learn to speak much earlier than five, it is only at that age or later that visual-to-auditory recoding ability develops. This conclusion is confirmed by Flavell, Friedrichs, and Hoyt (1970), who found that children in the second and fourth grades actively named pictures and rehearsed the names while trying to commit the names of the objects to memory, while children in nursery school and kindergarten exhibited such behavior much less frequently. Thus, the development of recoding and rehearsal strategies may be one of the changes underlying more general changes in intellectual ability in young children.

 Chapter 3

ATTENTION AND
ORGANIZATION IN MEMORY

In the last chapter, Peterson and Peterson's classic retention study was described. When three-letter sequences were presented one at a time and followed by a distracting subtraction task, less than one-tenth of the sequences were recalled correctly after an eighteen-second interval. Because the task of subtracting numbers interferes with the process of storing information in LTM, storage may be said to require attention.

This chapter is concerned with some further questions about storage and attention. One question is whether attention is an all-or-none process, or whether some tasks interfere more than others with long-term storage. A second question is whether attentional limitations of storage can be easily overcome. Special emphasis given to some information apparently makes it easier to remember. Some people have even tried to learn while sleeping. A final question is what role attention plays in memorization. One view is that the mere repetition of material imprints it in memory. Another view is that attention plays a role in organizing material, and such organization is responsible for increased recall.

Attention Demands of Storage

Tasks such as counting backward by threes are known to interfere with the storage of information in LTM. Posner and Rossman (1965) wondered whether the attention required to store information varied with the difficulty of the interfering task, or whether it were an all-or-none phenomenon. They presented a series of five digits which were to be recalled ten seconds later. Following the presentation, a number of other digits were presented which subjects were asked to ignore, record on paper, add members of (32 would yield 3 + 2 = 5), count backward by threes (from the last two of the five digits to be recalled), or classify pairs (into high-even, high-odd, low-even, and low-odd). Preliminary work showed these tasks to be of increasing degrees of difficulty in terms of the time required to perform them. In the experiment, however, subjects had exactly ten seconds to perform the interpolated task, regardless of its difficulty, and they were asked to perform as fast as possible. Despite the fact that all interpolated tasks were performed for the same amount of time, the more difficult the interpolated task, the less the recall of the five-digit series ten seconds later.

There are two theories to explain how an interpolated task causes forgetting from STM. One theory is that each item in the interpolated task has a certain probability of displacing an item in STM. A second theory is that the interpolated task prevents rehearsal of the material to be recalled, and therefore the material spontaneously decays from STM. The Posner and Rossman study supports the latter theory. The more difficult the interpolated task in their study, the fewer the interpolated items there were. In the ten-second interval, fewer classifications were made than additions, for example, yet classification caused more forgetting than did addition. But this raises the question of why the more difficult interpolated tasks interfered more with the learning task. Perhaps the more difficult tasks used by Posner and Rossman involve more mental operations than the simpler tasks, and those mental operations, because they require attention, interfere more with the storage operation of rehearsal, which also requires attention. It may be that each mental operation either requires attention or does not, in an all-or-none fashion, while a task may require more or less attention depending on the number of mental operations it involves.

The Von Restorff Effect

In any given number of items to be learned, an item that is notably different from the rest, because it is larger or of a different color or has some other differentiating characteristic, is more easily learned than the others This phenomenon is called the Von Restorff effect after one of its early investigators. It might seem that the Von Restorff effect is a handy trick for facilitating memory. It is possible, however, that much of the effect can be attributed to a redistribution of attention. If people pay more attention to the distinctive item, then, according to the interference definition of attention, other items should suffer in recall. The cued items may be rehearsed more and the noncued items rehearsed less. The total effect on recall may be no improvement at all.

As part of their study of the attention demands of memory, Posner and Rossman also examined the Von Restorff effect. They presented four pairs of digits for recall. Control subjects did nothing but attempt to recall the digits. In the experimental condition, one of the four digit pairs was first classified as high-even, high-odd, low-even, or low-odd, and then recall was attempted. The digit pair that had been classified was recalled better than the control digit pairs. The nonclassified items, however, were recalled less well than the control items. The more one thinks about some material to be remembered, the worse is recall of other material presented at about the same time. Thinking requires attention, but so does storage. If one process is emphasized, the other is neglected.

A study by Waugh (1969) also showed that the Von Restorff effect has detrimental effects on other items. When a list of words was presented, words accompanied by a tone were recalled better than words with no signals. The nonsignalled words were recalled less well than words in a list with no signals at all. Most important, the total number of words recalled was almost exactly the same for the list with signals and the list without signals.

A common printing device is to emphasize more important material by italics or larger print. Hershberger and Terry (1965) presented to eighth graders text material with all the material in black print in one case, and with important material in red print and less essential material in black print in another case. The important material was remembered better when it was color cued, but the less essential material was remembered less well. The total recall was the same in both cases. Although it may be worth while to increase retention of more important material, cueing does not improve memory, it merely redistributes learning.

The inference from these studies is that people rehearse cued items more than noncued items, but the evidence for that inference is indirect, depending on the observation that noncued items show a decrement during recall. Rundus (1971) directly tested this assumption. He asked subjects to say out loud the words they were thinking of while memorizing a list of words. When a few of the words were printed in red, those words were overtly rehearsed more often than the words printed in black. The black items showed a reduction in rehearsal.

Storage requires not only time but attention. When time is limited, attention can be distributed unevenly over different items, but the overall limitation on storage capability appears to be difficult to overcome. It is possible, however, that some part of the Von Restorff effect is due to an actual improvement in recall and not simply to a redistribution of attention. Proper cueing may improve the organization of material to be learned or may help differentiate some material from other thereby improving recall.

Learning during Sleep

As we have seen, memorizing while awake requires work. More interesting diversions can interfere with the task of committing information to memory. How nice it would be if we could postpone our more boring learning to a time of sleep. An ability to memorize information while sleeping could have important social implications; in Aldous Huxley's novel, *Brave New World*, learning during sleep was used to shape the beliefs of young children. Machines for learning during sleep have been commercially marketed. Recently, however, the attorney general of New York banned the sale of one company's language learning machine that purported to teach while the learner was asleep. It was claimed that there is no evidence for sleep-learning of language (*Consumer Reports*, 1970, p. 313).

The primary problem in determining whether memorization can occur during sleep is to determine whether the subjects are indeed asleep at the time information is presénted. The most definitive study on this issue was performed by Simon and Emmons (1956). During the night, while subjects were sleeping, ninety-six questions and answers were presented (for example: In what kind of store did Ulysses S. Grant work before the war? Before the war, Ulysses S. Grant worked in a hardware store.) To determine whether the subjects were actually asleep when a particular question-answer sequence was presented, subjects were asked to report whenever they heard the item. In addition, electroencephalograph (EEG) recordings of brain waves were continually taken and classified according to level of sleep.

When recall by the experimental subjects was compared with their pretest knowledge and with the knowledge of a control group, there was no evidence of learning during sleep. If subjects did not report hearing a question-answer sequence at the time it was presented, no learning occurred. If the EEG recordings indicated sleep below the level of conscious awareness at the time the question-answer sequence was presented, no learning occurred. Even a more sensitive multiple-choice test showed no evidence that material presented while sleeping was stored in memory.

To test the possibility that simpler information might be retained, particularly if it were repeated a number of times during sleep, Emmons and Simon (1956) presented ten different words as many as eighty-two times during periods in which EEG recordings indicated that subjects were asleep. In a recognition test the next day, there was no evidence that the information had been stored in memory.

The studies by Simon and Emmons indicate that verbal memorization is not possible during sleep. Reports professing to have found sleep-learning of verbal material usually have not been able to confirm by means of EEGs that subjects were actually asleep. Certain types of sleep-learning other than verbal learning are possible, however. Beh and Barratt (1965) presented either a high or a low tone during sleep. Initially the tones had no effect on brain activity as measured by the EEG. Then the low tone was regularly followed by a rather intense electrical shock, which elicited EEG activity referred to as the K-complex. Eventually the low tone as well as the shock came to elicit the K-complex. The high tone, which had not been paired with shock, remained neutral in its effect. This simple type of learning, referred to as classical conditioning, can thus occur during sleep. Furthermore, Beh and Barratt found that the response that was conditioned during sleep transferred to the waking state.

Weinberg (1966) demonstrated that another simple type of learning, operant conditioning, can also occur during sleep. When EEG recordings indicated the subject was sleeping, a mild shock was given to substantiate that the subject was indeed asleep. If no arousal occurred in response to the shock, either a high or a low tone was presented. When the high tone occurred, the subject was to close a switch with his hand, in which case he would receive twenty-five cents the next day. If the switch was not closed, a loud bell would wake him up fifteen seconds later. The low tone required no response. Over a few nights a week for several weeks, the subjects gradually learned to close the switch in response to the high tone.

Storage of verbal material in memory is apparently different from classical or operant conditioning. Storage of verbal materials requires attention in the sense of being awake and not being distracted by other tasks, but classical conditioning and operant conditioning may occur during sleep. In addition, Hefferline, Keenan, and Harford (1959) found that operant conditioning may occur while a subject is occupied with another task, such as listening to music. Electrical impulses were recorded from a tiny muscle twitch the subject was not aware of. When the twitch occurred, a hum, which had been mixed with music, was temporarily postponed. Eventually the twitch was conditioned to postpone the hum, despite the fact that subjects were not aware of either the muscle response or their own role in controlling the noise.

Before dismissing completely the possibility of learning verbal material while sleeping, some consideration of dreaming is needed. (See Berger 1970 for a recent discussion of dreaming and memory, and Grosser and Seigal 1971 for a review of current theories of sleep.) At various periods during sleep, the EEG changes considerably from a slow-wave state to a state partially resembling wakefulness, and the eyes move rapidly and irregularly. This state is called REM (rapid eye movement) sleep. For some time it has been known that dreams occur during REM sleep, since a person awakened at that time often reports having been dreaming. Most of these dreams are not recalled the next day, suggesting that they usually are not stored in LTM. Some dreams, however, are remembered the next day, and it thus appears that mental events can sometimes be stored while sleeping. REM sleep is quite different, however, from the type of sleep defined in the experiments discussed earlier. It is possible that no storage in LTM actually occurs in the REM state. Perhaps storage only occurs when people nearly awaken after a dream. We remember nightmares because they often wake us up.

Recently, it has been shown that mental activity also occurs during non-REM sleep, although it is usually less vivid and more abstract than REM dreams. Occasionally non-REM activity is remembered later. Because there is no way of knowing exactly when non-REM mental activity is occurring, the stage of sleep as assessed by an EEG at the time of the activity cannot be known. Consequently, it is not clear that remembering of non-REM dreams is possible in a deep stage of sleep.

There have been reports that verbal material presented during sleep may be incorporated into dreams that occur during REM sleep (see Oswald 1966, pp. 77–81, for a review of these reports). Sometimes the sound of the verbal material is apparently incorporated; other times the meaning is incorporated. Whether such modifications also can occur during non-REM sleep has not been investigated, presumably because of the difficulty of knowing when a non-REM dream is in progress.

Further studies on memory storage and retention of dreams may shed light on the possibilities of learning during sleep. Generally, however, storage of verbal material in LTM seems to require one's attention in the sense of being awake and free from interfering tasks.

Organization and Memory

Memorization has been shown to be an active process that takes time and that an irrelevant task can easily interfere with. This active, attentive process is called rehearsal. Two hypotheses have been proposed to explain why rehearsal improves memory. One hypothesis is that rehearsal is just a form of repeating an item to oneself; the more often an item is repeated, the more likely it is to be embedded in LTM in a form adequate for recall. A second, more interesting hypothesis is that mere repetition is not sufficient for memorization; rehearsal acts to organize material in memory, and without such organization repetition is useless. Practice makes perfect only if practice is used to organize.

A direct attempt to determine whether mere repetition of items is sufficient for memorization was made by Tulving (1900). A list of twenty-two nouns was prepared. An experimental group saw each word in the list on six occasions prior to being asked to memorize the words, and on each occasion they were asked merely to read the words. Nothing was said at that time about the necessity for later memorizing. A control group was similarly shown a prior list of words but these were unrelated to the words they would later memorize. Tulving found no differences between the two groups in their attempts at memorization and recall, suggesting that repetition is not sufficient for storage in LTM.

Some studies (such as that of Wallace and Calderone 1969) have found that subjects who merely repeat words aloud, without having been instructed to learn them, have improved recall. However, when learning occurs in the absence of instructions to learn, it is not always clear that repetition is the only factor involved. Subjects may have also attempted to organize the information, and organization may account for the better recall. Wallace and Calderone found that subjects who were instructed to repeat words, without knowing that they would later need to recall them, actually recalled the words in related clusters. For example, names of different plants in the list might be recalled in a cluster.

The implication is that subjects not only repeated words as instructed but also mentally organized them.

In another experiment, Tulving (1962) was interested in the order in which subjects recalled a list of items. He presented sixteen unrelated words one at a time and then asked subjects to try to recall the words in any order. After one presentation of the list, only about six of the words were recalled, but, as would be expected, further trials led to better performance, until by the sixteenth trial about fifteen words were recalled. The improvement in recall with increasing number of trials is shown in figure 11.

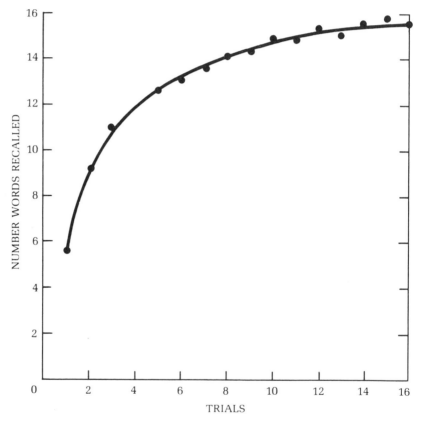

Figure 11. Improvement in free recall of a list of words over trials. (Data from Tulving, 1962)

Tulving suggested that the improvement in recall was due to increasing organization in storage. To test this hypothesis, he developed a measure of subjective organization (SO) that gauges the degree of consistency in recall. The more often the words are recalled in the same order from trial to trial, the higher the SO. As shown in figure 12, SO also increased with increasing number of trials in a parallel manner to improvement in recall. Although subjects were free to recall the words in any order they chose, they tended to recall the words in similar orders on successive trials even though the presentation order was different from trial to trial. In other words, improvement in recall was accompanied by a structure imposed by the subjects on the list of apparently unrelated items.

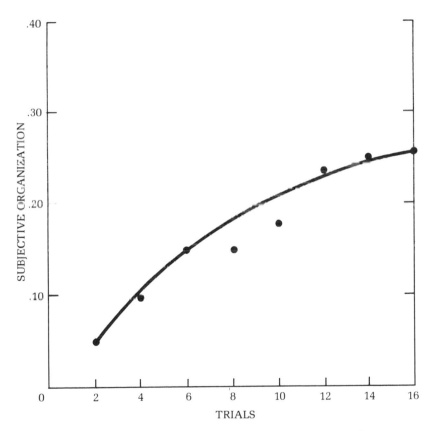

Figure 12. Subjective Organization increases at the same time that recall improves. (Data from Tulving, 1962)

One reservation must be noted in interpreting the results of Tulving's study. A correlation between increased recall and increased SO does not prove that SO is necessary for improved recall. To establish a causal connection, it is necessary to manipulate experimentally the degree of organization and observe its influence on learning. Information with a readily apparent organization that fits in with previous learning should be much easier to store than material with no obvious structure. Dallett (1964) argued that if organization is the critical factor controlling recall, then words that fall into natural categories (such as *peas, carrots, lettuce, corn;* and *Brazil, Germany, Australia, Canada*) should be better remembered than a list of unrelated words. Further, the items composing natural categories should be recalled better when the items within a single category are presented in blocks rather than mixed with items from different categories. As expected, categorized lists were recalled better than unrelated words, particularly when the category items were presented in blocs.

The data from Tulving on SO and from Dallett on categorization and recall suggest that attention and rehearsal actively organize material in memory. Rundus (1971) directly observed this process of organizing by asking subjects to say out loud whatever words they were thinking of while memorizing. He found that when a word from one category was presented (such as *pea*), a word from the same category that had been presented earlier (such as *carrot*) was very likely to be rehearsed at the same time. In their overt rehearsal, subjects bring related words together; related words are also usually recalled together.

Rehearsal strategies of the sort described by Rundus are not used to the same extent by everyone. Such strategies develop during childhood and may deteriorate in old age. Thus, changes in organizational strategies appear to be an important component in changes in memory capacity with age. Neimark, Slotnick, and Ulrich (1971) presented twenty-four pictures to children in grades one, three, four, five, and six and to college students. The subjects looked at the pictures placed before them for three minutes and were allowed to rearrange them at will. The pictures could be classified into four categories—animals, transportation devices, household furnishings, and clothing. The tendency to organize the materials in these categories increased in all cases from one age to the next. Even sixth graders did not organize as much as did college students. Furthermore, as age increased, the recall of the pictures from memory displayed increasing degrees of organization.

In a study of memory and aging, Laurence and Trotter (1971) compared free recall (recall in any order) of a list of thirty-six words by subjects averaging twenty-three years of age with that of subjects averaging seventy-five years of age. Of the thirty-six items, all of which were visually presented, twelve were acoustically unrelated, twelve were pairs of words with similar sounding names (such as *warning* and *morning*) and twelve were homophone pairs (such as *boarder* and *border*). Recall of such a long list would be primarily from LTM. As shown by the Kintsch and Buschke (1969) study, discussed in chapter 2, acoustic similarity has little or no effect on forgetting from LTM. It may, however, provide a basis for organization of material in LTM. Thus, it might be expected that if similar sounding words were grouped together rather than being distributed in different portions of the list, recall would improve because of the increased likelihood that subjects would use the organization. In fact, grouping of acoustically related material did improve recall for the younger group but not for the older group. A study by Craik (1971) found that older people did not differ from younger people in either STM or recognition of words that had been presented in long lists of words. Thus, it appears that memory deficits in the aged are mainly attributable to failure to utilize efficiently the existing organization in material.

If recall is a byproduct of organization imposed on a list of items, then situations in which information is highly organized might lead to good memory even if subjects are unaware that they will later be asked to recall the information. Such a situation can be compared with Tulving's repetition experiment, in which the material was not organized. In a study by Eagle and Leiter (1964), some subjects were told to categorize words as nouns, verbs, adjectives, and adverbs, but they were not told until after they had seen the words that they would need to remember them. These subjects actually recognized the words better when they subsequently saw them than did subjects who had been told to try to memorize the words but who had not been told how to organize them. On a recall test, however, the subjects who had been instructed to memorize the words did better. But further analysis showed that only those subjects who had been instructed to memorize the words and who also used an organizational strategy of their own were able to recall better than the uninformed subjects who used grammatical organization. Intention to learn is not as important as organization.

The Eagle and Leiter study found that organization improved recognition of previously presented material. However, recognition is considerably easier than recall, which requires that items stored in memory be retrieved without visual prompting. Some other studies, in contrast to the Eagle and Leiter study, have found that while organization is important for recall, it is not very important for recognition. Such results have led investigators to make a distinction between the storage of information and the accessibility of stored information. Presumably, information stored in memory can usually be recognized even when organization is poor, but it can only be efficiently recalled when it is stored in an organized fashion. The distinction between storage that permits recognition and storage that permits recall has been glossed over in this chapter. In summarizing the effects of organization on storage, it would therefore be more correct to say that mere repetition of words is not sufficient for recall. Good recall requires that rehearsal organize information. When a good organization is formed, one item can then prompt the recall of another. Organization of information in LTM is facilitated when the material fits in with previous knowledge of the subject. Thus, if a list contains words that can easily be organized into categories such as vegetables and countries, learning is much easier. When a natural organization is absent or not apparent, the subject must impose his own. In Tulving's 1962 study, apparently unrelated words were used. Subjects imposed a structure on the words by storing them in a very constrained order, so that they were recalled in approximately the same order on each successive trial.

Because material that has good natural organization is easier to store for recall than material with no apparent organization, it is important that material to be learned be well organized. One offshoot of learning research has been the development of programmed learning techniques. It has often been stressed that the important characteristic of programmed learning is the immediate reinforcement of a correct answer. It is possible, however, that success of such learning methods is due not to reinforcement but to the organization of the presentation. (See Cook 1963 for a critique of straight-forward applications of reinforcement principles.) If the principle of organization were taken into account explicitly, even better programs might be developed.

Imagery and Memorization

In a small, fascinating book, *The Mind of a Mnemonist*, the famous Russian psychologist, A. R. Luria (1968), describes some phenomenal memory feats of a subject referred to simply as S. S's capacity for memorizing material appeared to be unlimited either by the number of items or by the time span over which items were remembered. In fact, with the exception of a few very instructive errors, Luria was unable to demonstrate any forgetting at all with S. S could remember perfectly a list of nonsense material he had memorized perhaps fifteen years earlier. It did not matter whether the list was a few items in length or many. Not only was S able to remember the test material, he was also able to describe what the experimenter was wearing that day, where he was sitting, and so on. The only requirement for the outstanding memory feats of S was that at the time of original presentation he be allowed to study the material for three or four seconds.

The key to S's memory feats appeared to be imagery. As he was memorizing he might imagine, for example, a familiar street, and while mentally walking along the street place images of objects to be recalled in various places along the way—on houses, on gates, in windows, and so on. To recall the items, S had merely to "walk" along the street again mentally and observe what had been placed in each position. This example indicates how visual imagery may improve memory; it is a very potent device for organizing information so that none of it is missed. S could systematically retrace his steps to be sure that he recalled each item.

Was imagery really necessary for S's phenomenal recall, or was it just an incidental accompaniment to a perfect memory? The few errors that S made seemed to be attributable to his having mentally placed a white object on a white background or in a dark passageway, for example. Thus, the error could be attributed to his not "seeing" the item during recall. In his later career as a professional mnemonist, S learned to avoid such errors by being careful where he placed items. Further evidence that the memory was visual was that he could recall material equally well either forward or backward or, for a table of numbers, diagonally.

Although most people would probably like to improve their memories, a highly detailed memory depending on imagery is not desirable in all respects. In S's case, the vivid imagery evoked by words interfered with his ability to abstract the meaning of a message, leading him to think about irrelevant details of his images rather than following the message. This problem seemed to interfere with most jobs he undertook, and so he eventually became a professional mnemonist.

Rules for Imagery

It is tempting to dismiss such impressive feats as those of S as special skills not attainable by most humans. Such a dismissal might be premature. While probably only a few people could duplicate S's performance, certain of his techniques, namely his imaginal and organizational techniques, might be used by others. In fact, over two thousand years ago in the book *Ad Herennium* by an unknown author, some very explicit rules for memorization were formulated, and they bear striking resemblance to those used by S. Some of the rules included in Yates's (1966) translation of *Ad Herennium* follow:

> If we wish to remember much material we must equip ourselves with a large number of places. It is essential that the places should form a series and must be remembered in their order, so that we can start from any *locus* in the series and move either backwards or forward from it.
> . . . The formation of the *loci* is of the greatest importance for the same set of *loci* can be used again and again for remembering different material.
> . . . In order to make sure that we do not err in remembering the order of the *loci* it is useful to give each fifth locus some distinguishing mark. . . . It is better to form one's memory *loci* in a deserted and solitary place for crowds of passing people tend to weaken the impressions. . . . Memory *loci* should not be too much like one another, for instance too many intercolumnar spaces are not good, for their resemblance to one another will be confusing. They should be of moderate size, not too large for this renders the images placed on them vague, and not too small for then an arrangement of images will be overcrowded. They must not be too brightly lighted for then the images on them will glitter and dazzle; nor must they be too dark or the shadows will obscure the images. [Pp. 7–8]

Besides rules for the loci, techniques used in forming the images to be placed in loci are described as follows:

> When we see in every day life things that are petty, ordinary, and banal, we generally fail to remember them, because the mind is not being stirred by anything novel or marvellous. But if we see or hear something exceptionally base, dishonourable, unusual, great, unbelievable, or ridiculous, that we are likely to remember for a long time. . . . Thus, nature shows that she is not aroused by the common ordinary event, but is moved by a new or striking occurrence.

> . . . If we set up images that are not many or vague but active (*imagines agentes*); if we assign to them exceptional beauty or singular ugliness; if we ornament some of them, as with crowns or purple cloaks; . . . or if we somehow disfigure them, as by introducing one stained with blood or soiled with mud or smeared with red paint, . . . or by assigning certain comic effects to our images . . . that, too, will ensure our remembering them more readily. [Pp. 9–10]

The principles of *Ad Herennium* are of two types: organizational and image construction. An orderly sequence of places (loci) in which to store the material to be remembered is needed. This provides the framework for recall. Rules for image formation stress the use of the unusual—features that stand out. These principles were probably developed not on the basis of experimental data but from personal experience.

Experimental Studies of Imagery and Memory

Before examining studies attempting to determine why imagery facilitates memory, two basic questions must first be answered. One is whether imagery itself improves memorization or whether the long time involved in constructing images accounts for improvement in memory. The second question is whether imagery should be considered to be visual.

In an attempt to answer the first question, Bugelski, Kidd, and Segman (1968) taught experimental subjects the "one-is-a-bun" mnemonic technique. This technique requires, first, the memorization of ten words rhyming with numbers one through ten (see table 1). Suppose the first item to be remembered is *telephone*. Then one might imagine a bun with a telephone in it and a person taking a bite of the bun. (*Bun* is always used for the first item, since it rhymes with *one*.) If the second item to be remembered is *horse*, one might imagine a horse standing in some tennis shoes ("two is a shoe"). In recall, one thinks of the number, then the associated rhyming word, and finally the associated image.

Table 1

Rhyming Words Used As a Mnemonic Device

One is a bun
Two is a shoe
Three is a tree

Four is a door
Five is a hive
Six is sticks
Seven is heaven
Eight is a gate
Nine is wine
Ten is a hen

After learning the rhyming scheme and being instructed in its use, experimental subjects were shown word-number pairs for two, four, or eight seconds per pair. Control subjects, although they had learned the rhyming scheme, were told nothing about using it in the subsequent memory task. With two-second presentations, there was no difference between the two groups in success of recall. At four- and eight-second presentations, however, the experimental group showed superior recall. Given enough time to construct images, imagery does seem to facilitate recall independent of rehearsal time.

To explore the question of whether or not imagery involves the visual system, Atwood (1969, 1971) presented thirty-five word pairs embedded in image-evoking phrases (such as *hen* pecking a *book*). As in Brooks's experiment described in chapter 2, Atwood reasoned that if, upon reading the phrase, subjects constructed visual images, then recall should deteriorate more upon subsequent presentation of a visual task than upon subsequent presentation of an auditory task. His results supported that inference. Recall of word pairs embedded in more abstract phrases (such as, the *intellect* of Einstein was a *miracle*) deteriorated more when an auditory task was presented immediately following each phrase than when a visual task was presented. Thus, it appears that imagery does involve the visual system.

The reports of Luria's subject S and the historical rules from *Ad Herennium* suggested that imagery alone is not sufficient for improving recall; imagery must be accompanied by organization. To test that notion, Atwood (1969), in another study, led subjects through his laboratory, noting various places (such as doorways and desks) that could later be used for memorization. Subjects in one group were then asked to mentally put images of various objects to be recalled in the different places in the laboratory (a knife on the desk, for example). Presumably, those subjects would be able to recall the information stored by mentally retracing their steps through the laboratory and recalling the objects in the different places. Control subjects were also told to construct images, but the places in which they mentally put the objects were not organized in any particular way (they imagined a knife sticking in the ground, for example). The group that put the images in places in the laboratory did much better in recall than the control group.

It appears quite clear, therefore, that an important aspect of successful recall technique is an organizational framework in which to place images. In addition, the nature of the images themselves are important. Atwood found that if people were asked to imagine printed, abstract words (such as *metaphysics*) in different locations instead of imagining objects, recall was very poor. Good organization of poor images is not sufficient for good recall.

Images of objects can, of course, be constructed in many ways. What features of image construction result in good recall? Classical rules suggested that images should be bizarre. But Atwood found bizarreness to make no difference in recall. "Gorilla swinging an axe" is no better remembered than "empty matchbook." Atwood suggested that when bizarreness is useful for memory, it may be because bizarre images are more interesting to create than are mundane images. Consequently, people may spend more time creating bizarre pictures in their minds. The finding that bizarreness has no effect on recall under conditions controlled for time has also been reported by Bower (1970).

If bizarreness is not important in image construction, what is? Atwood found that organizational factors are important in image construction as well as in construction of the loci. Mere juxtaposition of objects (such as a *truck* driven by a *nudist* who stands near a lead *pipe*) results in poorer recall than when the objects are related to each other in some manner (such as, *truck* being attacked by a *nudist* with a lead *pipe*). Horowitz, Lampel, and Takanishi (1969) showed three- and four-year-old children pictures such as those in figure 13. Some of the pictures were unified as on the left side of the figure. Others were not unified, as on the right side. Twenty seconds after the presentation, a picture with two of the objects was shown, and the child was asked to name the missing object. Children recalled the missing object from unified scenes better than they did from those that were not unified.

Exactly what constitutes unity in an image is not clear, but apparently imagery by itself is not a great aid to recall. The images must be well structured, they must be mentally placed in an organized framework that will guide recall, and time must be taken to develop an image. When images are properly constructed, as they are in many pictures, they are remarkably resistant to forgetting. Shepard (1967) compared recognition of pictures from a long list of pictures with recognition of words from a long list of words. The pictures were retained much better.

Figure 13. Unitary and non-unitary pictures of objects such as those used by Horowitz, Lampel, and Takanishi. The objects in the left panel were remembered better than those in the right panel.

Organization and Memory of Less Specific Information

So far, the discussion has been concerned with memory for rather specific items. Memory for specifics is undoubtedly an important part of everyday life. We remember names, telephone numbers, things to get at the grocery store, and so on. But certainly these examples are not representative of most of what we remember. We read books, attend movies, and talk to friends. We do not remember all the individual utterances or words involved in these activities or even all the word meanings. Instead, as Pompi and Lachman (1967) have shown, we remember something like the general idea, theme, or overall meaning. The difficulty of defining an idea or overall meaning, however, poses a problem for research on this type of memory. How can one study a phenomenon as difficult to measure as the theme of a passage of writing? Perhaps it is because of this problem that most research has been based on memory for specific material. This is not to say, however, that research on storage of specific material is not useful for understanding memory for less specific material. For instance, understanding the meaning of a sentence often depends on relating earlier parts to later parts of the sentence, and this, in turn, depends on STM.

One technique for measuring meaning was recently developed by Dawes (1964), who suggested that meaning is essentially a statement of logical relationships between elements. The meaning of a story is retained if the logical relationships are retained, regardless of whether different words or word arrangements are used in recall. The task of the learner is to organize the material in memory in such a manner that the critical relationships are maintained.

According to Dawes, the various relationships can be classified into four types, examples of which are given in figure 14. In

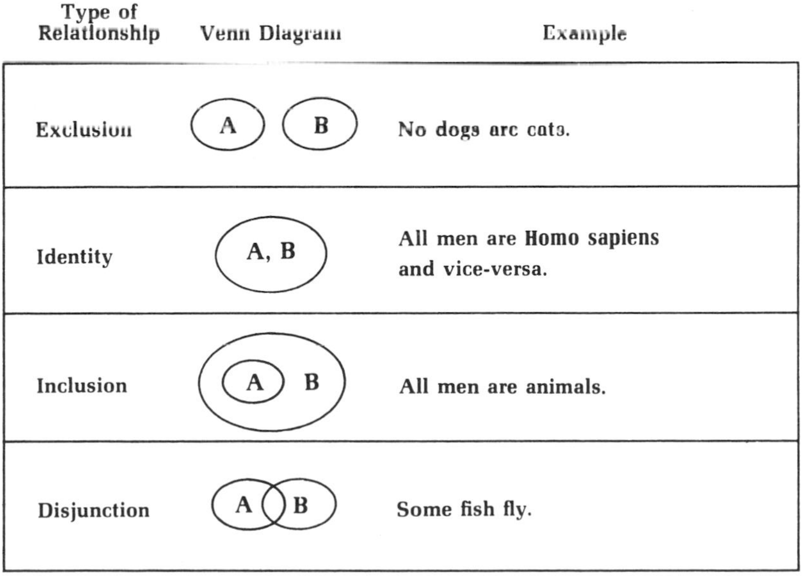

Type of Relationship	Venn Diagram	Example
Exclusion	(A) (B)	No dogs are cats.
Identity	(A, B)	All men are **Homo sapiens** and vice-versa.
Inclusion	(A) B	All men are animals.
Disjunction	(A∩B)	Some fish fly.

Figure 14. Logical relationships between elements.

an *exclusion*, no members of one class belong to another class. An *identity* relationship involves complete overlap of the two categories. In an *inclusion*, all members of one class belong to another, but not vice versa. Finally, in a *disjunction*, some but not all members of one class belong to another and vice versa.

A disjunction is more complex than the other relationships in that it involves finer discriminations, or more categories. To say that some but not all Russians are Communists, and to say that some but not all Communists are Russians is to make a finer discrimination than to lump everything together by saying, "all are," or "all are not." For this reason, Dawes grouped exclusions, identities, and inclusions together. If a story includes one of these relationships and a person remembers it as a disjunction, then he has made a *pseudodiscrimination*—that is, he has made a finer distinction than is warranted. For instance, if a certain disease has always been fatal (an inclusion of the disease class in the broader class of fatalities), but a person afflicted with the disease feels that he will live, then he is making a pseudo-discrimination; he has created a disjunction by placing himself outside the category of fatalities. The converse, to change a disjunctive relationship to a simpler form, is to *overgeneralize* (by saying, for example, that all Russians are Communists).

To apply these notions in an actual test situation, Dawes constructed the following story for subjects to read (a Venn diagram of the story is shown in figure 15):

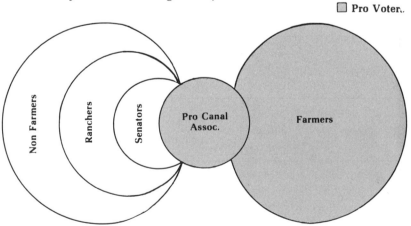

Figure 15. A Venn diagram of the relationships among the principal elements of "Circle Island."

Circle Island is located in the middle of the Atlantic Ocean: it is a flat island with large grass meadows,

good soil, but few rivers and hence a shortage of water.
The main occupations on the island are farming and
cattle ranching. While the majority of the islanders are
farmers, the ranchers are much more prosperous, for
they are less affected by the lack of water; thus, no
ranchers farm in addition.

The island is run democratically; all issues are decided
by a majority vote of the islanders. The actual govern-
ing body is a 10-man senate, whose job is to carry out
the will of the majority. Since the most desirable trait
in a senator is administrative ability, the senate consists
of the 10 best proven administrators—the island's ten
richest men. For years, all the senators have been
ranchers.

Recently, an island scientist discovered a cheap method
of converting salt water into fresh water; as a result,
some of the island farmers wanted to build a canal
across the island, so that they could use the water from
the canal to cultivate the island's central region. Some
of the farmers formed a pro canal association and even
persuaded a few senators to join.

The pro canal association brought the idea of con
structing a canal to a vote. All the islanders voted, with
all the members of the pro canal association and all the
farmers voting for construction and everybody else voting against it. The majority voted in favor of construc
tion.

The senate, however, decided it would be too dangerous to have a canal that was more than 2 in. wide and
3 in. deep. After starting construction on such a canal,
the island engineers found no water would flow into it,
and the project had to be abandoned.

After reading the story, subjects were asked to choose the correct alternative from pairs of statements, one of which implied
a disjunctive relationship and the other a nondisjunctive relationship. One pair, for example, was (1) No ranchers voted for
construction of the canal; and (2) Not all, but some ranchers voted
for construction of the canal. Notice that the correct alternative
(the second) was not stated in those words in the story, yet the
relationship it implies was presented.

The results were clear cut. When errors were made, they were
errors of overgeneralization more often than errors of pseudodiscrimination. In later work, Dawes (1966) found no tendency for
such simplification to increase over longer retention intervals of
two days. However, the subjects actually showed no forgetting
at all over a period of two days as compared to immediate recall,

perhaps because recall was so poor in the immediate situation. Further work in which forgetting is found to increase over time might show a tendency toward greater simplification.

The importance of Dawes's work lies not only in its demonstration that meaningful material is remembered in a simplified form but also in its development of a methodology for analyzing the retention of highly complex material. The method is essentially a description of the organization of the elements in a story. The difficulty of memorization depends on the degree of organization of the material to be learned.

Summary

Unfortunately, perhaps, memorization is a difficult process. Although we may wish that we could remember things without paying attention to them or while concentrating on other things, Posner and Rossman have demonstrated that this is not possible. Memorization requires not only time but also attention.

Improved memory for cued items (the Von Restorff effect) usually occurs to the detriment of memory for other items. In addition, people cannot memorize verbal material while sleeping. Simple classical and operant conditioning are the only types of sleep-learning so far demonstrated, and the range of application of these techniques is certainly limited. The fact that people can sometimes remember dreams, however, indicates that our knowledge of sleep-learning is not complete, and it is possible that sleeping can be exploited for more complex learning.

To say that storage requires attention is to say that the mental processes required by demanding tasks interfere with some process involved in storage. The storage process that requires attention is called rehearsal. One hypothesis is that rehearsal improves memory in the absence of other, interfering mental operations, simply by virtue of mental repetition. But experiments by Tulving have shown that mere repetition does not facilitate recall. Recall improves only when the material to be learned is organized, and such organization in memory is facilitated when the material is structured by the experimenter or teacher. In the absence of such structure, the learner must impose his own. The rehearsal process is used to rearrange information into an organized form for storage. A potent technique for organizing material so that none of it is missed in recall is the use of visual imagery. One way of organizing material through visual imagery is the "one-is-a-bun" technique. Another is the method in which images of objects to be recalled are mentally placed in familiar, organized locations. The construction of the images of objects themselves is also important. More important than bizarreness of image is that the various objects in an image be unified. However, no general statements about the kinds of relationships that yield unity of image have yet been formulated.

Most work on memory has been concerned with the retention of very specific material. Yet, typically, people remember themes or meaning rather than actual words. This deficit in research is due in part to the difficulty of measuring meaning. Dawes has suggested that the meaning of a passage is essentially embodied in the relationships that exist among the elements of the passage. By classifying relationships as exclusions, inclusions, identities, and disjunctions, and by analyzing types of recall errors made, Dawes has shown that people tend to make more errors of overgeneralization than of pseudodiscrimination.

What can you do to improve your memory? Rehearse, organize, and image. When a person is introduced to you, repeat his name to yourself several times and try to relate it to something else. When you try to memorize a list, actively organize it. If you want to recall what you read, organize it with respect to other material you have learned and make clear all the relationships that exist between its elements. A mnemonic scheme such as the method of loci will help you store material that requires exact recall.

Chapter 4

THE MEASUREMENT OF INFORMATION

Information is conveyed by events, including words, pictures, movements, tones, and so on. When information is stored in memory, retrieved, and results in a movement, it is said to have been processed. Some information is more difficult to process than other information. Visual information persists a shorter time in sensory storage than does auditory information, making sequential material such as Morse code easier to process from auditory input. A word list organized in a way that is consistent with past learning is easier to store than a list that does not take advantage of previous learning. Unified images are easier to store in memory than nonunified images. A factor not previously discussed that also influences processing difficulty is the predictability of an event. Highly probable events make for easier information storage and retrieval than do less probable events. Because the predictability of events has a very strong influence on processing efficiency, it is useful to quantify information in terms of probability.

This chapter describes a method of measuring information that takes predictability into account and discusses experiments that have used the measurement techniques. Some of the studies concern storage of information in memory, and some concern the discrimination of stimuli that occur in isolation from other stimuli. The next chapter describes the application of information measurement methods to retrieval time. Information measurement, in addition to being useful for understanding of psychological processes, has also been used to describe other systems such as ecological systems (to assess, for example, the degree to which pollution simplifies and makes more predictable an ecosystem) and to describe the capacity of a computer to handle the load imposed by a user.

Information and Probability

The amount of information conveyed by an event is directly related to the uncertainty of that event. A highly probable occurrence, such as the rising of the sun, conveys little information that was not already known. Comparatively unpredictable events, like eclipses, convey much more information. To take another example, a list of twenty digits would convey less information per item (and presumably be easier to memorize) than a list of twenty letters, because with only ten possible items there is less uncertainty than with twenty-six possible items.

The amount of information conveyed by an event is equivalent to the number of questions that would have to be asked to accurately predict the event's occurrence. The greater the uncertainty of the event, the greater the number of questions necessary, and the greater the information it conveys. Suppose that there are sixteen lights arranged in a four by four square. The probability that any particular light will be turned on is one-sixteenth. Suppose further that you are to guess which light will be turned on by asking questions that can be answered either yes or no. Only four such questions are needed: Is the light in the top two rows? No. Is it in the bottom row? No. Is it in the two left columns of the third row? Yes. Is it in the left-most column? No. Only one possibility remains—the second light from the left in the third row from the top. Because only four questions were needed to identify which one of sixteen possible events would occur, there are said to be four bits of information in each of the events. (The term *bit* is an abbreviation of *binary digit* and implies that each answer to a yes-or-no question is coded as a 0 or a 1.)

If the number of possible events were increased, each event would be less probable, more questions would be needed to determine which event would occur, and the information conveyed by the event's occurrence would be increased. Varying the number of possible events is only one way of varying the amount of information they convey. The number of possible events can remain fixed, and their probability of occurrence can be altered. Let us return to the example of the sixteen lights. If you know that there is a 75 percent probability that a light in the top row will be turned on, your line of questioning will be modified. You will first ask whether the light is in the top row. If the answer is yes, you have only two remaining questions. If the answer is no, you have four more. The illumination of lights in the top row thus conveys less information than the illumination of lights in the other three rows.

Mathematical Representation of Information

Two demands must be satisfied by a quantitative measure of information. First, the information quantum should increase as the probability decreases. Second, the information quantum should increase in proportion to the number of questions that would be needed to predict an event's occurrence. In particular, when the probability of an event is reduced by half, the information should increase by one bit, because one additional question would be needed for prediction. One measure that satisfies these requirements is

$$H_i = \log_2 \frac{1}{P_i}.$$

Let us examine this equation to see if it meets the two requirements. H_i is a symbol for the amount of information, in bits, conveyed by a particular event, i. P_i is the probability that event i will occur in a given situation. As P_i becomes smaller, the value $1/P_i$ becomes larger; likewise $\log_2 1/P_i$ becomes larger. The requirement that information (H_i) increases as probability (P_i) decreases is therefore satisfied; information is greater the more uncertain the event. The logarithmic feature of the equation satisfies the requirement that when the probability is reduced by half, H_i should increase by one bit. Table 2 helps explain the logarithmic feature. The top row of the table lists the number of possible events ranging from a situation of only one possible event to a situation of eight possible events. (The particular numbers of possible events were chosen because their logarithms are whole numbers.) The second row shows the probability of event i, assuming that each of the possible events is equally probable. The third row shows the number of events in exponential form. Thus, eight events is equivalent to the number two raised to the third power ($2 \times 2 \times 2 = 8$). The logarithm (base two) of any given number of events is simply the exponent shown in the third row of the table. The fourth row shows the logarithm, which is the amount of information. From this table it can be seen that each time P_i is reduced by half, the information increases by one bit.

Many events have probabilities different from those shown in table 2. For example, in a learning situation any of twelve possible words might occur in a certain list position. As seen from table 2, the amount of information conveyed would be more than three bits and less than four bits. Table 3 shows the amount of information for probabilities ranging from 0.01 to 1.00.

Table 2   Amount of Information Conveyed by Different Numbers of Equally Probable Events

Number of possible events	1	2	4	8	16	32	64
P_i (probability of event i)	1	1/2	1/4	1/8	1/16	1/32	1/64
Number of events in exponential form	2^0	2^1	2^2	2^3	2^4	2^5	2^6
$H_i = \log_2 (1/P_i)$ (bits of information)	0	1	2	3	4	5	6

Average Amount of Information

The notion of an amount of information conveyed by an event makes sense only when that event is viewed with respect to a set of related events. An infinite variety of events can conceivably occur, but in certain contexts the events of interest are very limited in number. The information one stores in memory regarding purchases at the grocery store is quite restricted. Another set of events is of interest to someone driving on a busy highway. Because in particular situations people are faced with sets of related events, it is often of interest to determine the average amount of information conveyed by those events. An aircraft controller continually responds to many signals. We may want to know not how difficult it is to process one signal from one aircraft but the average processing difficulty spread over a period of time. To determine average difficulty, we need to know the average amount of information conveyed by the different events.

When each of several events is equally likely, the average amount of information is the same as the amount of information of any individual event. Thus, in the example of sixteen equally probable lights, the amount of information conveyed by any given light was four bits. The average amount of information was also four bits. But when some events in a set are more or less probable than others, the average amount of information may be different than the amount of information of any one of the events. Suppose that in a given task three possible signals can

Table 3   Values of Log_2 $1/P_i$ and P_i Log_2 $1/P_i$ for Different Values of Pi

P_i	Log_2 $(1/P_i)$	$P_i \text{Log}_2$ $(1/P_i)$	P_i	Log_2 $(1/P_i)$	$P_i \text{Log}_2$ $(1/P_i)$
.01	6.644	0.664	.51	.971	.4954
.02	5.644	.1129	.52	.943	.4906
.03	5.059	.1518	.53	.916	.4854
.04	4.644	.1858	.54	.889	.4800
.05	4.322	.2161	.55	.863	.4744
.06	4.059	.2435	.56	.836	.4684
.07	3.836	.2686	.57	.811	.4623
.08	3.644	.2915	.58	.786	.4558
.09	3.474	.3127	.59	.761	.4491
.10	3.322	.3322	.60	.737	.4422
.11	3.184	.3503	.61	.713	.4350
.12	3.059	.3671	.62	.690	.4276
.13	2.943	.3826	.63	.667	.4199
.14	2.836	.3971	.64	.644	.4121
.15	2.737	.4105	.65	.622	.4040
.16	2.644	.4230	.66	.599	.3957
.17	2.556	.4346	.67	.578	.3871
.18	2.474	.4453	.68	.556	.3784
.19	2.396	.4552	.69	.535	.3694
.20	2.322	.4644	.70	.515	.3602
.21	2.251	.4728	.71	.494	.3508
.22	2.184	.4806	.72	.474	.3412
.23	2.120	.4877	.73	.454	.3314
.24	2.059	.4941	.74	.434	.3215
.25	2.000	.5000	.75	.415	.3113
.26	1.943	.5053	.76	.396	.3009
.27	1.889	.5100	.77	.377	.2903
.28	1.836	.5142	.78	.358	.2796
.29	1.786	.5179	.79	.340	.2687
.30	1.737	.5211	.80	.322	.2575
.31	1.690	.5238	.81	.304	.2462
.32	1.644	.5260	.82	.286	.2348
.33	1.599	.5278	.83	.269	.2231
.34	1.556	.5292	.84	.251	.2113
.35	1.515	.5301	.85	.234	.1993
.36	1.474	.5306	.86	.218	.1871
.37	1.434	.5307	.87	.201	.1748
.38	1.396	.5304	.88	.184	.1623
.39	1.358	.5298	.89	.168	.1496
.40	1.322	.5288	.90	.152	.1368
.41	1.286	.5274	.91	.136	.1238
.42	1.251	.5256	.92	.120	.1107
.43	1.218	.5236	.93	.105	.0974
.44	1.184	.5211	.94	.089	.0839
.45	1.152	.5184	.95	.074	.0703
.46	1.120	.5153	.96	.059	.0565
.47	1.089	.5120	.97	.044	.0426
.48	1.059	.5083	.98	.029	.0286
.49	1.029	.5043	.99	.014	.0140
.50	1.000	.5000	1.00	.000	.0000

occur, signals A, B, and C. Suppose further that signal A occurs one-half of the time $(P_A = \frac{1}{2})$, signal B occurs one-third of the time $(P_B = \frac{1}{3})$, and signal C occurs the rest of the time $(P_C = \frac{1}{6})$. The amount of information conveyed by the three events is

$$H_A = \log_2 \frac{1}{P_A} = \log_2 \frac{1}{.50} = 1 \text{ bit,}$$

$$H_B = \log_2 \frac{1}{P_B} = \log_2 \frac{1}{.33} = 1.585 \text{ bits, and}$$

$$H_C = \log_2 \frac{1}{P_C} = \log_2 \frac{1}{.17} = 2.585 \text{ bits.}$$

Notice that the less probable an event, the more information it conveys. When an event occurs, the probability is one-half that it is event A. On the average, over many events, therefore, the information contributed by event A is one-half multiplied by the information of A—that is, $1/2 \times 1$ bit $= .50$ bits. Likewise, since B occurs one-third of the time, on the average it contributes $1/3 \times 1.585$ bits $= .528$ bits of information, and C contributes $1/6 \times 2.585$ bits $= .431$ bits. In symbolic terms, the average amount of information, $\bar{H}$, in this situation is

$$H = P_A \log_2 \frac{1}{P_A} + P_B \log_2 \frac{1}{P_B} + P_C \log_2 \frac{1}{P_C} = 1.459 \text{ bits.}$$

In general, for any number, N, of possible events, the average amount of information is

$$H = \sum_{i=1}^{N} P_i \log_2 \frac{1}{P_i}.$$

To simplify the calculation of average information, table 3 shows the values of $P_i \log_2 (1/P_i)$ as well as the values of $\log_2 (1/P_i)$. The average information can be calculated by finding, for event i, the value of $P_i \log_2 (1/P_i)$ and adding the values for all events together.

For a fixed number of events, the average information is greatest whenever the various events occur with equal probability. Whenever some events are more probable than others, the average amount of information they convey decreases. This conclusion demonstrates the advantages of formulating information as a logarithmic function. Common sense tells us that, when we know that events are not equally probable, we have a better chance of predicting what will happen, and therefore the events convey less information on the average.

There are three basic ways in which amount of information can be manipulated, and limitations in dealing with events may be determined not so much by the manner in which information is varied as by the average amount of information conveyed. Those ways of varying the average amount of information are to vary the number of events that can occur; to make some events more probable than others; and to make the order in which events occur partially predictable. For example, there are twenty-six letters in the English language. If average information per item is an important factor in storing material in memory, letters should be more difficult to memorize than digits, since there are only ten digits. Some letters in the English language, such as *t* and *e*, occur more frequently than others, such as *x* and *z*. A list of letters that reflects these probabilities might be easier to learn than a list in which each letter occurred with equal probability because the average amount of information would be less in the first case. Finally, since letters tend to occur in certain sequences in the English language (the letter *h* follows *t* with a high probability, whereas *t* follows *h* with a low probability), a list reflecting probable sequences would further reduce the average information per item, and the reduction in information could facilitate storage.

Applications to Memory Research

Information essentially measures the amount of organization of events. Suppose, for example, that a list of letters must be memorized in a particular order. At one extreme, the letters could all be different. Each successive letter, therefore, would convey considerable information. At the other extreme, there could be only two different letters, each repeated a number of times in the list, yielding only 1 bit of information each. Such a list would be more highly organized than a list in which all letters were different. Some letters could also occur more often in a list than others, or they could tend to occur in certain sequences. These repetitions would represent increased organization in that they would make successive events more predictable.

Since the task of storing information in LTM is facilitated by organization of the material, the more information in a list, the greater should be the demand on the subject to organize the list in memory. On the other hand, the less the information, the more organization is inherent in the list, the less the demand on the subject to impose his own organization. If information is an important determinant of storage difficulty, smaller amounts of information should be easier to learn. Furthermore, it might be predicted that the time required for memorization would depend on the average amount of information and not on the manner of varying information (that is, number of different items, probabilities of different items, and sequential dependencies).

Both these predictions are supported by an experiment by Adelson, Muckler, and Williams (1955). Subjects learned lists of fifteen letters composed of two, four, six, or fifteen different letters. In some lists, the different letters appeared about equally often. In other lists, some letters appeared more often than others. Still other lists had approximately equal numbers of each letter, but certain letters tended to follow certain other letters when repeated in the list. These three types of lists are called balanced, unbalanced, and sequentially dependent. As seen in figure 16, the number of learning trials required until a list could be recalled without error increased with the amount of information it conveyed. Different ways of varying the information resulted in the same function. This is strong evidence that storage in LTM is limited by the degree of organization required, which in this case is measured by information.

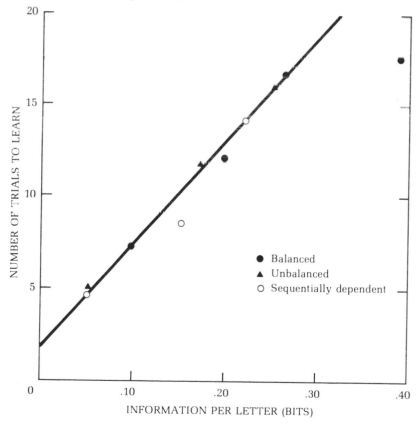

Figure 16. The average number of trials taken to learn a list of 15 letters occurring with balanced, unbalanced, or sequentially dependent probabilities. (Data from Adelson, Muckler, and Williams, 1955)

The Adelson, Muckler, and Williams experiment required complete recall of the entire list. The list was too long to be recalled completely from STM, so it had to be repeated a number of times until it was stored in LTM. In an immediate recall test, the items are presented only one time at a rapid rate, and the subject is asked to recall as many items as possible. With only one presentation, there is usually not sufficient time to store the material in LTM, and recall success is based primarily on STM. It was implied earlier that STM does not utilize organization. Consequently, the number of items recalled in an immediate memory test should be relatively independent of the average amount of information. Such a result was found by Hayes (reported in Miller 1956). Hayes compared recall of lists of two digits (1 bit per item), decimal digits (3.32 bits per item), letters (4.70 bits per item), letters and digits (5.13 bits per item), and monosyllabic words (about 10 bits per item). Figure 17 shows that about the same number of items could be recalled regardless of the amount of information per item. The slight advantage for low-information items can be explained by assuming that it is due to some small amount of recall from LTM.

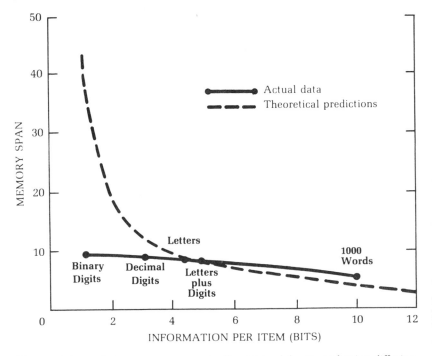

Figure 17. Immediate memory span actually obtained for items having differing amounts of information and theoretical recall where immediate memory dependent on the amount of information. (Revised from Miller, 1956 from data of Hayes)

The evidence that average amount of information affects LTM much more than STM supports the evidence presented in chapter 2 that STM and LTM are different processes and confirms the notion that storage in LTM depends on organization. Other evidence indicates that at least some types of organization do not influence STM. Craik and Levy (1970) presented subjects with a list of twenty words to be recalled immediately after presentation. The only restriction on the order of recall was that subjects attempt to recall the last few words first. Recall of words presented last in a list is, of course, heavily dependent on STM, although some items may have already entered LTM. Recall of items presented in the middle of the list is primarily dependent on LTM, however, since STM for these words will have deteriorated by the time of recall. In a control case, the twenty words were relatively unrelated to each other. In the experimental case, the sixth through eleventh items were all from the same category (such as *stomach, ankle, shoulder, muscle, kidney,* and *elbow*). The six related words were recalled much better than the comparable unrelated words, supporting evidence reported in chapter 3 that organizational factors are important in LTM. In a third case, the last six items in the list (the fifteenth through twentieth items) were related, and these items were also recalled better than the control items. However, when the proportion of recall due to STM was estimated by subtracting the proportion of recall due to LTM, STM did not appear to have benefitted from the organization.[1] The conclusion that organization is important for LTM but relatively or entirely unimportant for STM is consistent with the findings on the effect of amount of information on recall.

There has been much confusion about the effects of information on memory. Apparently contradictory results have led some investigators to discontinue using information measurement techniques to study memory. Much of the confusion can be cleared up, however, by considering whether recall is dependent primarily on STM or on LTM. Since recall from LTM is heavily dependent on organizational factors and recall from STM is not, the effects of information fit with our other knowledge of memory processes.

For those who want to pursue the study of the effects of information on immediate recall, one caution should be mentioned. Some data, such as that of Miller and Selfridge (1950), show considerable effects of the amount of information on immediate re-

---

[1]The proportion of recall for the last six items that is due to LTM is estimated from the proportion of items correctly recalled in positions six through eleven when STM is assumed to have deteriorated.

call of lists of words. The amount of information was manipulated by varying the degree to which the strings of words approximated English sentences. These results appear to contradict the claim that average amount of information has little effect on STM. But it must be remembered from Murdock's (1961) work that STM is limited by the number of meaningful units of material and not just by the number of items. Because of their prior familiarity with the English language, subjects could probably group successive words into larger units of meaning. In the experiment by Hayes described earlier, subjects were not instructed to group successive items into larger units. When they are taught to do so, immediate memory improves (see Miller 1956). Organization with which people are not already familiar does not aid STM, although it may aid storage in LTM. But material that is organized into units that are already meaningful also facilitates STM.

Transmission of Information

When a change occurs in a person's environment, he receives input of information. People also put out information when they respond to changes in their environments, and, to the degree that the output corresponds to the input, information is said to be transmitted. A skilled typist who receives information from a dictaphone, processes the information, and emits a pattern of responses highly correlated with the input has transmitted information. A young child may also listen to the dictaphone and peck the keys, but if there is no correspondence between the input and output, no information has been transmitted. At one extreme, when there is a unique response for each item of input and when no errors of response are made, all the input is transmitted. At the other extreme, when the output bears no relationship to the input, no information is transmitted at all. And when some errors are made by responding inconsistently to the input, some but not all of the information is transmitted. The measurement of information transmitted therefore is critical in determining the limits of information processing. It is not sufficient to examine only the input or the output; the degree of correspondence between the two must also be determined.

There are also many situations in which no errors are made but not all information is transmitted. These situations involve information reduction (see Posner 1964a). Much information from the environment may be irrelevant to the task at hand, and therefore it may be gated out. Teletype machines often type only capital letters, allowing letter case to be ignored. The reduction in the amount of information transmitted makes the task easier. In condensation tasks, none of the input is ignored, even though there are fewer responses than stimuli. The subject might combine two different stimuli, such as 4 and 5, into a single response, such as 9. Also, different stimuli may result in the same response, even though no information is gated, again reducing the amount of information transmitted from input to output. The additive combinations 4 + 5 and 6 + 3 both lead to the response, 9. Condensation that involves combining two stimuli into a single response may be more difficult the greater the information reduction. It may be recalled from the Posner and Rossman study (1965) that classifying two-digit numbers into four response categories was more difficult than adding them. Since adding yields nineteen possible responses, there is less condensation than in classification. Condensation in which several stimuli result in the same response is easier than transmission of all the information, however (Keele 1970). It is therefore important, when determining processing difficulty, to consider the type of information processing as well as the amount of information transmitted.

Measuring Information Transmitted

Two hypothetical examples will be useful to demonstrate how the amount of information transmitted is calculated. Suppose that letters on a conveyor belt are sorted by pressing two buttons. Letters with zip codes ending in 1 or 2 require that button A be pressed, and letters with zip codes ending in 3 or 4 require that button B be pressed. Table 4 gives frequency-of-response results for two operators. Both operators receive the same number of letters of each kind—ten out of every hundred letters end in zip code 1, twenty end in 2, thirty end in 3, and

Table 4   Hypothetical Frequencies of Letter-Sorting for Two Operators

Response

| | OPERATOR X | | | | | OPERATOR Y | | | | |
| | Zip Code (Stimulus) | | | | | Zip Code (Stimulus) | | | | |
	1	2	3	4	Total	1	2	3	4	Total
A	10	20	–	–	30	7	15	2	6	30
B	–	–	30	40	70	3	5	28	34	70
Total	10	20	30	40	100	10	20	30	40	100

forty end in 4. Thus, both operators receive the same amount of input information. Similarly, the amount of output information is the same for both operators; each presses button A thirty times and button B seventy times out of every hundred responses. Despite the fact that the amounts of input and output information are the same for the two operators, operator X transmits more information because he makes no errors, while operator Y makes several. Note that of the eight possible combinations of stimulus and response, only four occur for operator X. Although the same four combinations occur most frequently for operator Y, the remaining four also occur occasionally. Observation of the frequencies of different combinations of stimulus and response is critical for calculating the amount of information transmitted.

For a given number of stimuli and a given number of responses, a certain number of stimulus-response combinations are possible. If all the possible combinations occur with no tendency for some stimuli to yield some responses and other stimuli other responses, no information is transmitted. If, however, only the correct combinations occur, or if one stimulus tends to yield one response and another stimulus tends to yield another response, then some information is transmitted. In the letter-sorting example, eight combinations of four stimuli and two responses are possible, but some of them are incorrect. For instance, when zip code 1 is presented, response B is an error. Only four combinations of zip code and response should occur for maximum information transmittal.

To calculate the amount of information transmitted, the maximum possible amount of information of the various stimulus-response combinations is calculated. This value increases when either the stimulus information or the response information increases and is equal to $H_s + H_r$, where H_s represents the total amount of information conveyed by the stimuli and H_r the total amount of information conveyed by the responses. Then the *actual* information of the stimulus-response combinations, $H_{s,r}$, is calculated from the probabilities of each of the combinations. If $H_{s,r}$ is as large as $H_s + H_r$, that is, if all the combinations of stimulus and response actually occur with no predictability between the stimulus presented and the response emitted, then no information is transmitted. However, if some combinations of stimulus and response predominate, so that $H_{s,r}$ is less than theoretically possible, then some information is transmitted. The information transmitted, H_t, is therefore equal to the maximum possible information of the stimulus-response combinations minus the actual information of the stimulus-response combinations, or

$$H_t = (H_s + H_r) - H_{s,r}.$$

Let us apply this formula to the two examples. For operator X, the four zip codes occur with probabilities of 0.10, 0.20, 0.30, and 0.40. Therefore, $H_s = 0.10 \log_2 (1/0.10) + 0.20 \log_2 (1/0.20) + 0.30 \log_2 (1/0.30) + 0.40 \log_2 (1/0.40) = 0.3322 + 0.4644 + 0.5211 + 0.5288 = 1.8465$ bits. Likewise, the response information, $H_r = 0.30 \log_2 (1/0.30) + 0.70 \log_2 (1/0.70) = 0.5211 + 0.3602 = 0.8813$ bits. In this example, $H_{s,r}$ is the same as H_s, since four of the stimulus-response combinations occur with the same probabilities as the four stimuli, and the other combinations do not occur. The information transmitted from stimulus to response is therefore $H_t = (1.8465 + 0.8813) - 1.8465$, or 0.8813 bits. The information transmitted in this example is less than the input information, not because of errors but because there are fewer responses than stimuli. The information transmitted cannot exceed either the input information or the output information.

For operator Y, the input information is the same as for operator X; $H_s = 1.8465$ bits. H_r is also the same as for operator X: 0.8813 bits. But $H_{s,r}$ is equal to $0.07 \log_2 (1/0.07) + 0.03 \log_2 (1/0.03) + 0.15 \log_2 (1/0.15) + 0.05 \log_2 (1/0.05) + 0.02 \log_2 (1/0.02) + 0.28 \log_2 (1/0.28) + 0.06 \log_2 (1/0.06) + 0.34 \log_2 (1/0.34)$, or 2.4468 bits. Therefore, $H_t = (1.8465 + 0.8813) - 2.4468$, or 0.2810 bits. As expected, less information is transmitted by operator Y than by operator X.

Application to Absolute Judgments

If items of information are to be stored in memory, they must be differentiable one from the other. Different memories can be stored about different people, for instance, only if one person can be distinguished from another. The discrimination of an item as being distinct, when it is isolated from other, similar items, is called *absolute judgment*. Hundreds of values can be discriminated on a single dimension such as hue or tone pitch when stimuli are presented side by side for comparative judgment. But many fewer stimuli can be discriminated when other stimuli are not present for comparison.

A basic problem in analyzing a person's capacity for absolute judgment is the manner of handling errors. As the number of items to be distinguished increases, a point will be reached at which some errors are made but overall performance remains good; the errors are close approximations of the correct answer. One way of handling errors is to calculate the amount of information transmitted. The question then becomes whether there is a limit to the amount of information that can be transmitted in absolute judgments.

Many experiments on absolute judgment are summarized by Attneave (1959), Garner (1962), and Miller (1956). In all of them, subjects were shown values that varied on a single dimension, and they responded by attempting to give the correct name. The response given to each stimulus was then tabulated, a stimulus-response table was constructed, and the amount of information transmitted from stimulus to response was calculated. For all dimensions studied, as the number of stimulus values increased, the amount of information transmitted increased to between 2 and 3.5 bits and then remained constant or decreased. Absolute judgment is quite limited indeed. People can identify only about four degrees of saltiness without error (2 bits), six sound frequencies (2.5 bits), nine color hues (3.1 bits), and ten positions on a line (3.3 bits). When the number of values on a dimension increases beyond these limits, errors are made, and the amount of information transmitted remains about the same.

With such narrow limitations on absolute judgment, how are people able to discriminate so many things? Certainly, people can discriminate more than six or eight similar things. One possibility is that extending the range of values on a dimension increases the amount of information transmitted. Pollack (1952) had subjects discriminate tones differing in frequency. When the frequencies were drawn from the range of 100 cycles per second to 500 cycles per second, only about 1.8 bits of information were transmitted. When the range was extended almost twenty times, from 100 cycles per second to 8000 cycles per second, hardly any change occurred in the amount of information transmitted; only 2 bits of information were transmitted. It might be expected that if 2 bits of information were transmitted in a frequency range below 250 cycles per second, and 2 bits of information were transmitted in a frequency range above 2000 cycles per second, then combining the two sets of ranges would lead to 4 bits of information transmitted. However, when two such sets were combined by Pollack, the amount of information transmitted remained at 2 bits. Regardless of the spacing of tones, only four or five can be discriminated without error.

The Pollack results are extremely surprising. The general finding was confirmed by Eriksen and Hake (1955), however, who asked subjects to judge the size of squares. When the length of the sides of the squares varied from 2 millimeters to 42 millimeters, 1.84 bits of information were transmitted. When the range was doubled, with sides varying from 2 millimeters to 82 millimeters, the amount of information transmitted did increase to 2.01 bits, but the magnitude of the increase is small indeed. However, subjects in the Pollack and in the Eriksen and Hake studies had only small amounts of practice. Although extensive practice has little effect on increasing the amount of information transmitted when stimuli are regularly distributed over a range of values, practice could conceivably increase the amount of information transmitted when stimuli are not regularly distributed over a range of values.

Another possible explanation of people's ability to discriminate hundreds of things in everyday situations but many fewer values in experimental situations is that everyday objects typically have many dimensions; they differ not only in hue but also in saturation, brightness, three-dimensional shape, size, and movement. Everyday objects also exhibit a variety of sounds and have other properties, such as hardness, that make them discriminable.

A number of studies have shown that people can transmit much more information when the stimuli are multidimensional. Egeth and Pachella (1969), for instance, showed that when subjects identified positions of dots that could vary both horizontally and vertically, they transmitted a total of 5.84 bits of information on the two dimensions. (This is equivalent to being able to recognize about fifty-seven different positions.) This value, however, is less than double the amount that can be transmitted on a single dimension. For dots that varied in position only on the horizontal or only on the vertical dimension, 3.39 bits of information were transmitted.

It has consistently been found that the total amount of information transmitted for multidimensional stimuli, although much greater than that for single dimensions, is less than the sum of the amounts transmitted for single dimensions. Egeth and Pachella showed that the failure of such additivity is due in part to the fact that subjects had insufficient time to deal with the increased number of dimensions. When exposure time of the dots was increased from two to ten seconds, there was considerable improvement in two-dimensional information transmission. For stimuli such as salt and sugar concentrations, however, variation on one dimension interferes with the ability to judge the other, and two-dimensional information transmittal is less than would be predicted on the basis of unidimensional transmission, even when the stimuli are exposed for a relatively long time.

Summary

The concept of information measurement encompasses not just the occurrence or nonoccurrence of events but also their probability of occurrence. Not all information is equally difficult to process. The information conveyed by more probable events is often handled more efficiently than the information conveyed by less probable events, regardless of the cause of the increased predictability. Moreover, the difficulty of an overall processing task often depends on the average amount of information conveyed by all the events concerned. Material that requires several repetitions to memorize seems to be stored more easily when the average amount of information is small than when the average amount of information is large. In contrast, material which is recalled immediately after a single presentation, when STM is presumably the dominant process, is little influenced by the average amount of information but depends more on the total number of items. LTM is seen to depend on organization, here defined as information.

A second, useful function of information measurement is that it provides a method of measuring the efficiency of performance when errors occur. When information transmission measures are applied to absolute judgments, it is found that people are remarkably limited in the number of unidimensional values they can discriminate. Most people are able to discriminate only about eight color hues without error, for example. As the number of values becomes larger, the amount of information transmitted remains constant. This limitation on the number of values discriminable by absolute judgment is countered by the fact that most everyday discriminations refer to multidimensional things.

More extensive reviews of the formal measurement of information can be found in Attneave (1959) and Garner (1962). In Garner's book, *Uncertainty and Structure as Psychological Concepts*, the notion of information measurement is extended to specify kinds of organization as well as degrees of organization.

 Chapter 5

TIME AND ATTENTION FOR RETRIEVING INFORMATION FROM MEMORY

Information, once stored in memory, can be retrieved and used in interacting with the environment. Although sources of information may be retrieved and combined in making complex decisions, a person's efficiency in interacting with his environment is limited by the amount of time and attention it takes to retrieve the information. Skill in the game of basketball, for example, depends partly on how rapidly a player can retrieve from memory information about appropriate action in a particular situation. It also depends on what else the player can perceive and act on at the same time that he is retrieving information from memory. Not only physical skills but the process of thinking in general depends on retrieving and assembling information from memory. Efficiency of thinking may therefore depend in part on the time and attention required by the retrieval process. This chapter is concerned with the basic variables that influence time and attention of retrieval. The known effects of these variables are used to evaluate some theories about retrieval.

The study of retrieval time and attention makes great use of the reaction time (RT) technique and related techniques measuring, for example, the time required to sort or categorize a group of stimuli. RT is simply the amount of time that elapses between the onset of a signal and the onset of response to the signal. The actual movement time of the response is excluded, as far as possible. Response to a signal typically requires that information be drawn from memory, since there is nothing innate to the nervous system that requires a key to be pressed in response to a light, for example. It is for this reason that RT is said to reflect retrieval time. Of course, other factors also enter into RT—the time required for the sensory apparatus to become responsive, the time required for neural conduction to and from the brain, and the time required for a response to be initiated. Conclusions about retrieval time are therefore more meaningful when different degrees of retrieval complexity are studied so that the effects of retrieval time itself can be isolated.

The RT technique was first invented in the mid-1800s by Helmholtz (see Woodworth 1938) in an attempt to determine speed of nerve conduction. Helmholtz applied weak electrical shocks to the skin at varying distances from the brain, expecting that the further the distance, the longer would be the RT. On this basis, he estimated nerve conduction to proceed at about sixty meters per second.

It soon became obvious that the RT technique is more useful for measuring the amount of time required for mental operations, since mental operations require more time than neural conduction. In 1868, Donders compared RT to a single signal with RT to one of five possible signals, where each signal required a different response. He found that the average simple RT (in the single-signal case) was 197 milliseconds, and the average choice RT was 285 milliseconds, about 90 milliseconds more. This was the first demonstration that the time necessary to make a decision, even a well-practiced decision, depends on the number of alternative stimuli and responses that can occur in a situation.

The value of simple RT found by Donders is fairly representative. Many studies have shown that simple RT to auditory or tactual stimuli averages about 160 milliseconds, and RT to visual stimuli, such as those used by Donders, is slightly slower, averaging about 190 milliseconds. Choice RT almost always takes longer. Thus, in any situation, people require at least one-sixth to one-fifth of a second and normally longer to react. On May 5, 1969, *Sports Illustrated* published the measured RT of the great heavyweight boxer, Muhammed Ali, in responding to a flash of light. Ali's RT, measured from the signal to the beginning of the movement, was approximately 190 milliseconds—about average. The 16 1/2 inch movement following RT was completed in only 40 milliseconds, however. This example suggests that the skill of a great boxer does not lie in his ability to react to an opponent's punch, since RT is considerably longer than the time required to execute the movement, but rather in his ability to anticipate a punch.

Donders's experiment demonstrated that choice RT is longer than simple RT. The question of whether RT depends on the number of choices then arises. Imagine that there are two signals (for example, colors) and two corresponding responses (for example, key presses). Suppose that a subject is given considerable practice in responding to signals 1 and 2, and then two more signals and responses are added. Will the additional signals and responses change the RT to signals 1 and 2? To determine this, Merkel in 1885 (see Woodworth 1938) presented subjects with varying numbers of digits to which they responded by pressing appropriate keys. The digits 1 to 5 were assigned to keys pressed by fingers of the right hand, and the Roman numerals I to V were assigned to the left hand. For different numbers of alternatives, the subjects knew exactly which stimuli were possible (for example, if there were two stimuli, they would be 3 and IV). Merkel's results are shown in table 5. For each increase in number of alternatives from which to choose, there is an increase in RT. This is quite a remarkable finding, considering that subjects were well practiced and knew exactly which stimuli would occur and which responses were appropriate.

Table 5   Number of Alternatives and RT

NUMBER OF ALTERNATIVES	RT (IN MILLISECONDS)
1	187
2	316
3	364
4	434
5	487
6	532
7	570
8	603
9	619
10	622

Information and Reaction Time

A closer look at Merkel's results shows that, although RT increases with the number of alternatives, the increase caused by adding an alternative is larger when there are fewer alternatives than when there are many. Thus, when there are nine alternatives from which to choose, the addition of another alternative increases RT by only 3 milliseconds, but when there is only one alternative, the addition of another yields a 129-millisecond increase. To look at the data another way, RT increases by an approximately constant amount (about 140 milliseconds) each time the number of alternatives doubles, implying that RT is a linear function of the logarithm of the number of alternatives. This suggests that RT is a function of amount of information conveyed by the choices to be made. Because information measurement was not developed until the late 1940s, it was not until the early 1950s that this implication of Merkel's data was explored. Hick in England and Hyman in the United States independently worked out implications of the information hypothesis for RT; their formulation is known as the Hick-Hyman law.

Hyman's Contribution

As pointed out in chapter 4, changing the number of events, as Merkel did, is only one way to vary the amount of information. Information can also be manipulated by varying the probabilities of the different events and by varying the sequential dependencies of successive events. Hyman (1953) did all three things. In one set of conditions, he varied the number of stimulus lights from one to eight. Each light was associated with a different verbal response, and the subject's task was to respond as rapidly as possible following the onset of a light. In another set of conditions, Hyman, while keeping the number of alternatives fixed, made some alternatives more probable than others. For example, in one four-light condition three lights each occurred with probabilities of one-sixteenth, and the remaining light occurred with a probability of thirteen-sixteenths; in another four-light condition one light occurred four-eighths of the time, a second light two-eighths of the time, and the remaining two each occurred one-eighth of the time. Finally, for a fixed number of alternatives, each light occurred equally often but with certain sequential dependencies. For instance, in a three-light condition, given that light A had occurred, there was an eight-tenths chance that light B would occur next and only a one-tenth chance that A would repeat and a one-tenth chance that C would occur next. Similarly, light C tended to follow B, and A tended to follow C.

The results for Hyman's four courageous subjects (each subject participated in more than forty sessions) are shown in figure 18. For all three methods of varying information, RT increased with amount of information. The more remarkable result is that RT is determined primarily by the amount of information and not by the manner in which it is varied. For all of Hyman's subjects, RT is a linear function of the amount of information:

RT $= a + bH$, where a and b are constants, and H is the amount of information.

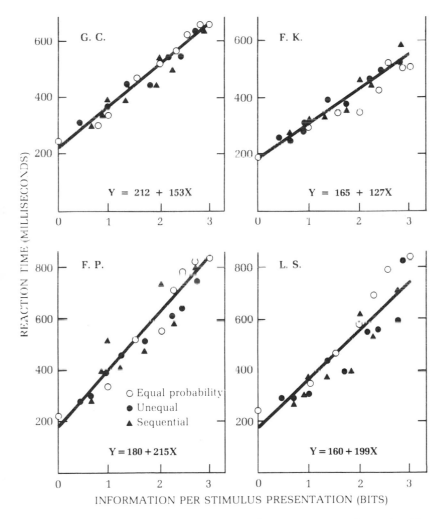

Figure 18. RT as a function of the average information in sets of stimuli with equal probabilities, unequal probabilities, and sequential dependencies. (From Hyman. 1953)

In verbal terms, when zero information is conveyed, RT is equal to the constant a, which ranged from 160 to 212 milliseconds for the different subjects. For each bit of information added, RT increases by a constant amount, b, which in different subjects ranged from 127 to 215 milliseconds.

There is no relationship between any person's a and b components. A person who has a small a may have a large, medium, or small b. The components seem to measure quite different aspects of the decision process. It is possible that a is a measure of quickness of the sensory and motor systems, while b reflects the efficiency with which information can be retrieved from memory. There has been no systematic study of the implications of individual differences on these components for the ability to perform different tasks. RT has not been found to bear a strong relationship to intelligence test scores. Perhaps the factoring of RT into memory and nonmemory components would yield a stronger relationship with intelligence.

Hick's Contribution

Suppose that, in an RT situation a subject is motivated to respond faster, perhaps by monetary rewards for fast responses and penalties for slow responses. There certainly is evidence that, when motivated, people can respond faster. But with a decrease in RT, there is an increase in number of errors. This is the well-known speed-accuracy trade-off.

The measurement of amount of information transmitted takes errors into account. The problem can be posed as follows: Imagine that there are eight equally likely stimuli—that is, three bits of input information—and that each stimulus is assigned a different response. Now suppose that with rapid responses so many errors are made that only two bits of information are transmitted. Is the resultant RT the same as the RT to four stimuli (two bits of input information) when no errors are made (two bits transmitted)?

In a classic study, Hick (1952) attempted to answer this question. In one condition, Hick himself responded to various numbers of alternative lights ranging from one to ten. Each light was assigned a different finger key, and when a light was illuminated, the corresponding key was to be pressed rapidly. Because very few errors were made, the information transmitted was essentially equal to the stimulus information, which ranged from 0 bits for one stimulus to 3.3 bits for ten stimuli. In another condition, ten lights and ten keys were always used, but Hick responded at different speeds. Information transmission was calculated from the errors made. For both conditions, RT was predicted by the same equation:

$$RT = a + bH_T,$$ where H_T is the information transmitted.

The constants a and b were the same in both conditions. According to Hick's results, the critical determinant of RT is not the number of stimuli and responses, but the amount of information transmitted. When errors are made and less information is thus transmitted, there is a corresponding decrease in RT, which is almost exactly equivalent to the RT that would be obtained in an error-free situation with the same information transmission. Speed is traded for accuracy, so that the rate of information transmission is constant.

The equation fitted to Hick's results is identical to that for Hyman's results, except that H_T is substituted for H. The Hick-Hyman law is rather remarkable in its range of applicability; in one simple equation it describes the effects of number of alternative stimuli and responses, unbalanced probabilities of events, sequential dependencies between successive events, and speed-accuracy trade-off. It has been pointed out by some (such as Kornblum 1969), however, that there are sometimes inconsistencies in the results. Sometimes RT is not as sensitive to changes in probabilities of different stimuli or sequential dependencies as to changes in number of stimuli. A close analysis of figure 18 shows some systematic departures from the fitted function. Some of these departures are eliminated, however, in more carefully controlled experiments (such as those of Hyman and Umiltà 1969; and Umiltà and Trombini 1968). Another problem is that certain factors other than amount of information transmitted also affect RT. Posner (1964a) pointed out that RT depends on the number of stimuli condensed into a single response, even though amount of information transmitted is constant when the number of responses is constant.[1] Morin and Forrin (1963) found that when more than one response is assigned to a single stimulus, RT increases, despite the fact that amount of information transmitted again remains constant. Finally, information measurement gives few hints about the processes that underlie decisions. Nevertheless, the Hick-Hyman law summarizes a considerable amount of data.

[1]Amount of information transmitted cannot exceed the amount of information in the input. Likewise, information transmitted cannot exceed the amount of information in the output. (See chapter 4.)

Compatibility and Practice

The Hick-Hyman law would be very useful, indeed, if by knowing how many stimuli and how many responses were possible, one could make exact predictions of decision time. It would be useful to engineers, for example, trying to design machines or to decide the spacing of highway signs. But in the same year as Hyman's work, Fitts and Seeger (1953) published a study indicating that there is no fixed value for decision time. Decision time depends on the relationship between stimuli and responses as well as amount of information.

The Fitts and Seeger study utilized eight stimuli and eight responses, but, as shown in figure 19, the stimuli and responses were of varying types. Stimulus set A involved eight lights arranged octagonally, and any of the eight lights could come on one at a time. Set B had four lights arranged in a diamond shape,

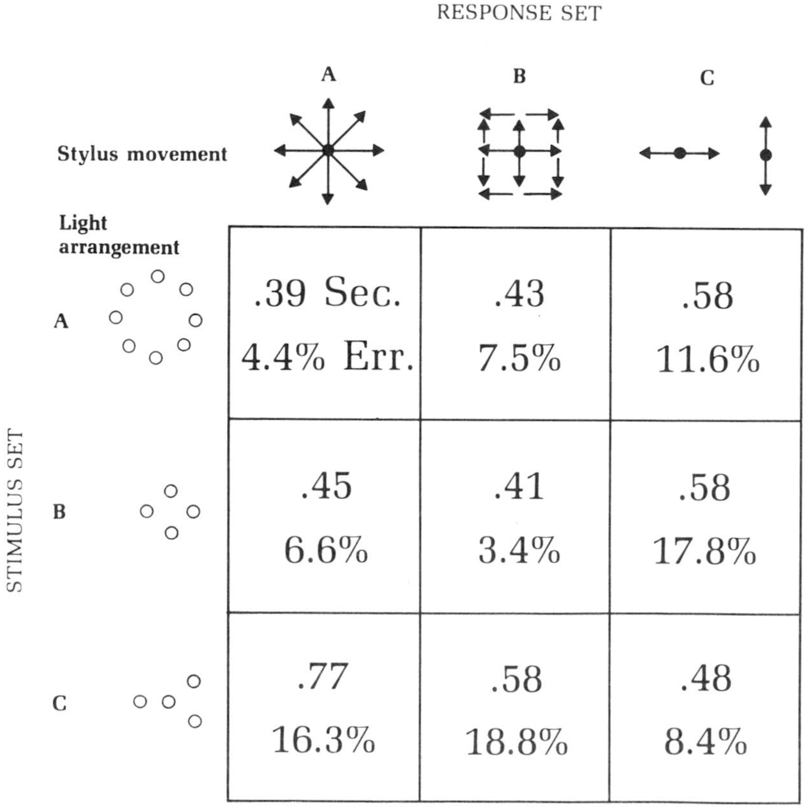

Stimulus set	Response set A	Response set B	Response set C
A	.39 Sec. 4.4% Err.	.43 7.5%	.58 11.6%
B	.45 6.6%	.41 3.4%	.58 17.8%
C	.77 16.3%	.58 18.8%	.48 8.4%

Figure 19. RT and percentage of errors for different combinations of stimuli and responses. (Revised from Fitts and Seeger, 1953)

and any one light could come on (four alternatives) or any adjacent pair of lights could come on (four more alternatives). For set C, there were again four lights, two in a horizontal line and two in a vertical line. Any of the four lights could come on alone, or any of the four combinations of one horizontal and one vertical light could occur. There were also three response sets. Subjects held one stylus for response sets A and B and two styluses for set C. The styluses were to be moved along tracks as illustrated in figure 19. In response set A, the stylus was started at the center and moved along one of eight tracks radiating outward like spokes on a wheel. Set B involved a grid pattern; the stylus could be moved, for example, up and then left. For set C, one hand could move one stylus up or down, and the other hand could move the other stylus left or right.

Each response set could be paired with each stimulus set. For example, with stimulus set A and response set C, a light on the upper left diagonal would require that one stylus be moved up and the other stylus be moved left. For each of the stimulus-response combinations, the RT and number of errors made are shown in figure 19. (Remember that RT is measured only until the beginning of movement and does not include the time of the movement itself.) The important result is that no one stimulus set resulted in the fastest time or least errors. Similarly, no one response set was best. Instead, the most important determinant of decision time and number of errors made was the relationship between stimulus and response. The fact that some stimulus-response relationships result in faster RTs than others is called S-R compatibility; the faster the RT, the more compatible the stimulus and response are said to be. Usually, the most compatible relationship is the one that a majority of people feel is the most natural.

The simple notion of compatibility is often ignored by machine designers. In World War II, there were many accidents by pilots attributable to incompatible arrangements of dials and controls. Fitts and Jones (1961) studied the errors that pilots made and suggested changes to overcome the incompatibilities. They cite the following illustration of bad design:

> This was a case of mistaking prop pitch controls for throttle controls in a C-47 while the pilot was flying a GCA. We were on the final approach at about 600 feet when we noticed an unusual sound in the engines. What had happened was that the pilot had taken hold of the prop controls and was using them for throttles. They were next to the pilot while the throttles were in

the center. This was a bad installation also, because the gauge for the props was on the right of the manifold-pressure gauge while the prop controls were on the left of the throttle controls.

The casual observer can notice many other examples of incompatible stimulus-response arrangements in everyday life. Such incompatibilities might not be so important if they could easily be overcome by practice, but Fitts and Seeger, in an extension of their study described earlier, found that even with thirty-two sessions of practice, the effects of incompatibility, though reduced, were not overcome.

Considering the importance of compatibility, two additional and related questions arise. One question concerns the minimum decision time that can be obtained with maximum compatibility. The second question concerns the effect of varying the amount of information under different degrees of compatibility. A study by Leonard (1959) is relevant to both these questions. He placed vibrators under either one, two, four, or eight fingers of subjects, who were to press down the finger vibrated. The RTs were 182, 226, 229, and 217 milliseconds, respectively. These RTs are very fast compared with those of more than a half-second found in the Hyman study (see fig. 18). Although there was a slight increase from the one-signal case to two-choice RT, there was no further increase when there were yet additional alternatives. Considering only the two-, four-, and eight-alternative cases, there is no violation of the Hick-Hyman law. The relationship between RT and information is still linear, but the constant b is essentially zero.

Further experiments by Brainard, Irby, Fitts, and Alluisi (1962) and by Hellyer (1963) found a variety of slopes relating information to RT. Some cases, such as key-pressing in response to numerals, yield steep slopes (large constant b in the Hick-Hyman law); others, such as key-pressing in response to lights with a high degree of spatial correspondence between lights and keys, give medium slopes; and still others, such as naming numerals, give near-zero slopes.

Another factor influencing RT is the amount of practice. As already mentioned, Fitts and Seeger found the negative effects of poor compatibility to be somewhat reduced by extensive practice. Several investigators (such as Mowbray 1960) have also found that the slope relating RT and information is small for the task of naming digits or letters, and this result seems most attributable to extensive practice. In a study by Mowbray and Rhoades (1959), the effects of practice on RT were explicitly examined. Initially, there was a small difference in the RT of key presses to lights favoring a two-choice situation over a four-choice situation. But after 42,000 responses, performance in the four-choice situation improved to equal that of the two-choice situation.

In all cases, however, the relationship between amount of information and RT is approximately linear. Although the Hick-Hyman law is not able to predict exactly what the decision time will be, since that time depends on compatibility and practice as well as on amount of information, the law still succeeds in predicting the uniformly linear relationship.

Models of Memory Retrieval

A number of variables have been seen to affect the time required to make a decision—the number of alternatives, the probabilities of occurrence of the different alternatives, sequential dependencies, speed-accuracy trade-off, compatibility, and practice. Once important variables and their effects are known, it is useful to develop models of the underlying processes involved. Many different models exist, but most fall into a few categories. Good technical discussions of many of the models are provided by E. Smith (1968). Less technical discussions of some of the main types of models are included here.

One major assumption of many models has been that RT reflects memory retrieval time. The fact that RT depends partly on S-R compatibility and practice does support this assumption. It is possible, however, that some of the RT results are not dependent on memory. Some models assume that the primary determinant of RT is the time necessary to identify a stimulus rather than the time necessary to retrieve information regarding appropriate responses.

One rather simple model of the decision process is the *direct hookup* model. According to this model, in the learning process each stimulus becomes associated with a unique response, so that a particular stimulus tends to evoke a particular response and no other.[2] A photocell assembly is an appropriate analogy. If a

---

[2]The term *response* does not necessarily refer to a specific movement, since any of several movements could constitute the same response. In most RT tasks, subjects learn to associate stimuli (such as lights) with responses (such as key presses). Once the light-key correspondence is learned, any of several types of movements would suffice; a person could use his left or right hand, he could place his fingers on the keys, or he could use one finger to jump from key to key. The primary problem is to remember what key to press, not how to press the key. A relevant experiment distinguishing the notion of response from actual movement is one by Attneave and Benson (1969).

red filter is placed over one photocell and a green filter over another, and different responses are associated with the different photocell outputs, then a red light would affect one assembly but not the other.

The direct hookup model must immediately be rejected because it cannot account for the fact that RT increases with number of alternatives. The response of the red photocell would not be influenced by the possible occurrence of other colors. With extremely large amounts of practice or a great deal of natural compatibility, however, the direct hookup model is appropriate. (See the data of Leonard 1959; Mowbray 1960; and Mowbray and Rhoades 1959.) As will later be seen, the direct hookup model is a special case of the logogen model.

According to another model, called *serial search*, a representation of each stimulus is stored in memory with a representation of its corresponding response. When a stimulus is presented, it is compared one at a time with stored representations until a representation is found that matches the stimulus. The corresponding response is then available and can be produced. Different versions of this model all yield the same prediction— each added alternative stimulus adds a constant amount of time to the search required for a match. In other words, it is predicted that $RT = a + bN$, where a and b are constants, and N is the number of possible stimuli. The experiments discussed earlier, however, have shown that the *logarithm* of the number of alternatives is linearly related to RT. The serial search model is not congruent with these data.

However, the serial search model does accommodate other data. Sternberg (1969) as well as others have shown that when subjects are required to determine whether a letter is in a memorized list, RT increases linearly with the number of letters in the list. Exactly why RT increases in a linear fashion in this type of situation, while in other situations it increases logarithmically, is not clear. One possibility is that, with small amounts of practice on a letter list, especially when the selected letters are a subset of the alphabet, search occurs in a serial manner.

The primary datum with which any general model of RT must deal is the finding that RT increases a constant amount each time the number of stimuli is doubled. One model proposed to account for this finding is the *serial dichotomous* model (Welford 1960), according to which a stimulus is identified by performing a series of tests on the input. Each test reduces the number of alternatives by half. Suppose that there are four stimuli each having two relevant values, such as a green square, a green circle, a red square, and a red circle. When one of these four stimuli is presented, it can be identified by two successive tests, one for color and one for form. Similarly, if a third dimension having two values were added, there would be eight stimuli, but only three tests would be needed to identify the correct stimulus. The number of tests, therefore, increases with the logarithm of the number of stimuli. The model can be further extended to account for probability effects by supposing that values that are more probable are tested before values that are less probable. In addition, the speed-accuracy trade-off phenomenon is explained by assuming that, under rapid conditions, not all the tests are made, and errors often result.

The serial dichotomous model accounts for much of the RT data. It has the further advantage of similarity to feature-testing theories about pattern recognition (see Neisser 1967). Pattern recognition theories often assume that patterns such as letters are recognized on the basis of their features. Each feature helps differentiate a given pattern, and all the features combined uniquely specify a pattern. Computer programs have been proposed to isolate the features of various patterns and use them for identification (see, for example, Uhr and Vossler 1963). Feature-testing models do not necessarily require that testing for features occur serially, though, as does the serial dichotomous model.

Despite its success in accounting for data, there are shortcomings of the serial dichotomous model. First, some stimuli, such as color hues, do not seem capable of dichotomization. Of the hues, red, orange, yellow, and green, what test would first narrow the choice to two colors without identifying the color in question? Second, how can the model account for S-R compatibility and practice effects? With very high degrees of S-R compatibility or large amounts of practice, the number of stimuli and responses have no effect. The primary determinant of an increasing RT function when the number of stimuli is increased seems to be not the time required to identify the stimulus but the time required to retrieve the correct response from memory.

Logogen Model

A number of investigators have proposed similar models that assume the primary determinant of RT to be the time required to retrieve information about the appropriate response from memory. To phrase the idea another way, when a stimulus occurs, there is conflict as to which of several responses should be made. RT is a measure of the time necessary to resolve the conflict. One of the first attempts to apply a response-conflict model to RT was by Berlyne (1957). A more modern version, the *logogen model*, was proposed by Morton (1969a) to explain errors made in word recognition after very brief exposures.[3] The model assumes that the occurrence of a stimulus activates information stored in memory. Morton has suggested the term *logogen*, derived from the Latin terms meaning "word birth," for linguistic information activated in memory by presentation of a word. Here the term is used in a more general sense for any unit of information activated in memory, including the name of the stimulus, the meaning of the stimulus, or an appropriate response to the stimulus. A logogen may, when activated, lead to mental operations, such as rehearsal or counting, or to immediate bodily movement.

The most critical assumption of the model is that the activity elicited in a logogen by a stimulus is superimposed on highly variable background activity. This assumption of a variable background is consistent with what is known about the nervous system. At a gross level, brain activity recorded from the scalp by an electroencephalograph exhibits irregular and rapid changes; at a more molecular level, individual neurons typically fire in the absence of known stimulation, and the rate of firing varies from moment to moment. The effects of stimulation on a logogen may therefore be assumed to vary with the background activity. A given level of activity could arise from either the background alone or from the background plus the specific stimulation. Of course, the higher the level of activity, the greater the likelihood that the activity in a logogen is due to presentation of the corresponding stimulus.

In addition to fluctuations in activity in the correct logogen, other logogens in the set of alternatives being considered also fluctuate in activity from moment to moment. Furthermore, the stimulus corresponding to one logogen tends to activate the logogen corresponding to another stimulus when the stimuli or responses are similar to each other. Consider a situation in which you are introduced to two people at a party. Later, you see one of the people and you struggle to recall the correct name. The

[3]The logogen model is a mathematical model of the decision process, derived from statistical decision theory. A thorough understanding of the model requires familiarity with the concepts of probability and statistical decision theory. The discussion here gives only an outline of the ideas behind the logogen model and the predictions it makes. Swets (1961) provides a good introductory article on statistical decision theory as applied to the detection of signals.

two names compete. The more similar the visual appearances of the two people, the more strongly the names compete, and the longer it takes to remember the correct name.

In general terms, the logogen model is a theory of how decisions are made in the face of "noisy" data. Suppose S_1, one of two possible stimuli, is presented. The presentation will activate *both* logogens L_1 and L_2, representing the two possible responses. On the average, L_1 has the stronger activity, but at any one moment in time, L_2 may be more active. How, then, is an error in responding avoided? The logogen model assumes that, when a stimulus is presented, activity is cumulated over time in all the logogens in the set being considered. The longer the cumulation process takes, the more likely it is that background variability will average out, and the more likely it is that the correct logogen will have the greatest accumulation of information. The longer the time that elapses between stimulation and response, therefore, the more likely it is that the response will be correct.

In this model, there is no fixed retrieval time. The time required to accumulate sufficient information to allow a decision having a certain degree of reliability depends on the relative strengths of the competing response tendencies. If the association between a stimulus and the correct logogen is strengthened, or if the associations to incorrect logogens are weakened, then the time required to respond will be reduced. Moreover, retrieval is never completed in an absolute sense. Instead there must be a criterion specifying what constitutes sufficient information to initiate a movement or perform a mental operation. If the criterion is lax, many errors are made; if it is stringent, fewer errors are made, but RT is lengthened. These two concepts—strength and criterion—are central to the logogen model, and retrieval time as reflected in RT depends on both factors.

Predictions from the Logogen Model

The logogen model is designed explicitly to account for the speed-accuracy trade-off demonstrated by Hick; the less stringent the criterion, the faster the RT, and the more the errors. The mechanism by which practice and S-R compatibility influence RT is also quite direct. Presumably, these variables affect the strengths of association between sensory input and the logogens; the stronger the correct association, the more the input to a logogen outweighs the inherent variability of the system, and the faster the RT. In the extreme, a very large amount of practice or high natural S-R compatibility reduces the model to the direct hookup model, in which RTs are not only very fast, but the number of alternatives has no effect on RT.

As the number of alternative responses increases, additional logogens accumulate information because of the increased number of competing logogens that must be considered. The chances are increased that an incorrect logogen will have the greatest accumulation of information at some point in time. The tendency toward increased error is countered by raising the criterion level and hence lengthening RT. Thus, RT, according to the model, should increase with number of alternatives. Furthermore, the effect of adding one competing response should be much greater when there are only two others than when there are seven or eight other responses.

Hyman has shown that it is not just the number of possible responses that determines RT, but also the probabilities of the different alternatives. When the probabilities are reduced by increasing the number of alternatives, the criterion must, according to the model, be adjusted. By assuming that the logogens associated with high probability events (whether because there are few alternatives or because there are many alternatives, some more probable than others) have, in general, low criteria, and the logogens associated with low probability events have high criteria, the effects of probabilities on RT are predicted. One further prediction that follows from this model is that a low probability event often results in an error, and a high probability event is almost always responded to correctly. These predictions have been confirmed by Fitts, Peterson, and Wolpe (1963).

The predictions of RT derived from the logogen model have been described in very general terms. More precise, quantitative predictions can be made, but they require that the model be translated into mathematical terms. For instance, while the model makes a qualitative prediction of a decreasing effect of additional alternatives on RT as the number of alternatives is increased, it remains to be seen whether it also predicts that the function will be logarithmic in form, or nearly so. Early work by Stone (1960) has shown that one quantitative version of the logogen model accurately fits much of the known data, including the logarithmic function.

Only some of the data accommodated by the logogen model has been discussed so far. Later in this chapter, the way in which the model can account for the effects of stimulus similarity will be described. The model can also be extended to cover cases in which more than one signal is processed at a time.

The Repetition Effect: Bypassing Memory Retrieval

A consistent finding reported in many RT studies is that the response to an event that is repeated is quicker than the response to an event that occurred earlier but was not the last one to occur. This phenomenon, called the *repetition effect*, was first reported in Hyman's (1953) classic study of information and RT. Figure 20 shows that RT is relatively fast to the second occurrence of a stimulus when no other stimuli intervene between two occurrences. The RT advantage of a repeated event is particularly marked when there are many possible stimuli.

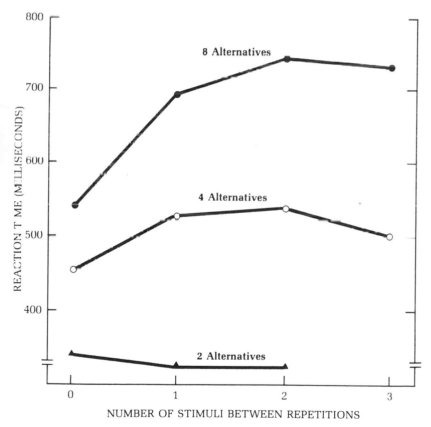

Figure 20. RT as a function of the number of alternative stimuli and the number of other stimuli that intervene between repetitions of a stimulus. (From Hyman. 1953)

One possible explanation of the repetition effect is based on the logogen model. When a stimulus occurs and a response is retrieved, there may be a temporary strengthening of the association between stimulus and logogen, which would decrease RT. However, the strengthening may decay over time. Keele (1969) found that increases in time between successive stimuli and even the insertion of an extraneous task between stimuli did not alter the repetition effect. Both M. Smith (1968) and Eichelman (1970) did find small decreases over time, but far from a complete disappearance of the repetition effect. The slight changes in the repetition effect over time occurred with relatively complex stimuli, suggesting that part of the repetition effect may be due to short-term sensory storage, which rapidly decays. The major part of the repetition effect shows no loss over time, however, implying that there is no temporary strengthening of the association between a stimulus and logogen.

An alternate explanation is that the repetition effect involves bypassing the retrieval stage. This notion was first suggested by Bertelson (1963), who proposed that when a stimulus occurs, the subject determines first whether the stimulus is the same as the previous one. If it is the same, then the subject makes the same response as previously; if it is not the same, memory must be searched to retrieve the correct response. It would be expected from Bertelson's hypothesis that the longer the retrieval time, the more time will be saved if a repeated stimulus is correctly anticipated and retrieval is bypassed. The time required to retrieve the correct response to a stimulus increases when either the number of stimuli and responses increases or the S-R compatibility decreases. Figure 20 shows that the more alternative stimuli and responses there are, the greater the savings in time by a repeated event. Further, Bertelson (1963) and Keele (1969) have shown a much larger advantage of repetitions over nonrepetitions for incompatible S-R arrangements than for compatible arrangements. These data, although consistent with Bertelson's hypothesis, are not conclusive proof for it.

Stronger evidence for the bypass notion comes from studies that have shown that, when subjects do not anticipate a repeated event, the repetition effect does not occur. Keele (1969) showed that when subjects verbally anticipated some event other than a repetition, then the RT for a repetition was not particularly fast. If the anticipated stimulus actually occurred, the RT was faster than normal. When LaBerge, Van Gelder, and Yellot (1970) cued subjects as to what stimulus might occur next, the cued stimulus showed a fast RT, and RTs to repetitions were hardly faster than those to other noncued stimuli. Finally, Keele and Boies (1972) found that when certain stimuli have high predictability because of sequential dependencies, repetitions having low predictability had RTs no faster than those to nonrepetitions.

The limitations that memory retrieval time place on the time required to respond to environmental change can be overcome by preparing in advance for a particular stimulus and response. Interestingly, however, only one event at a time appears capable of being anticipated. When there is no reason to anticipate a particular stimulus, people apparently notice when any stimulus is repeated. They then repeat their preceding response, thus saving retrieval time. But when there is a reason for anticipating a particular stimulus, as when one signal tends to follow another, then the more probable stimulus is anticipated, and repetitions lose most of their special status.

Stimulus Identification and Response Selection

A number of theorists (such as E. Smith 1968 and Welford 1960) have distinguished two substages within the general memory retrieval stage—stimulus identification and response selection. The theorists who distinguish these two substages have usually emphasized stimulus identification as being responsible for many of the results of RT experiments. For instance, the serial dichotomous model attributed the effects of amount of information to the stimulus identification stage of RT (see Welford 1960). Similarly, Smith's review of statistical decision theory, which in other respects is similar to the logogen model, emphasizes stimulus identification as being responsible for the effects of amount of information. As has been seen, however, some situations, such as key-pressing with a vibrated finger, or digit-naming, do not result in increased RT with increased number of alternatives. Since an increase in RT with an increased number of alternatives depends on the relationship between the stimulus and response, it appears more reasonable to attribute the effects of amount of information to retrieval of the appropriate response. Two phenomena have frequently been used to argue for the separation of the retrieval stage into the substages of stimulus identification and response selection—stimulus probability effects and stimulus similarity effects.

Stimulus Probability Effects

LaBerge and Tweedy (1964) showed that when two stimuli (such as red and blue) were assigned to one response, and another stimulus (such as green) was assigned to a second response, the more probable of the two stimuli sharing the same response resulted in faster RTs. Some investigators (such as Hawkins, Thomas, and Drury 1970; and Hinrichs and Krainz 1970) have argued, on the basis of similar results, that more probable stimuli are identified faster. The interpretation of the repetition effect suggests another explanation of the stimulus probability effect. Perhaps people tend to anticipate the more probable stimulus and, in anticipation, retrieve from memory the appropriate response. If the stimulus does occur, the response can be elicited without going through the retrieval stage. But if some stimulus other than the anticipated one occurs, then the time-consuming memory retrieval stage must take place. It may thus be the case not that the stimulus is identified more quickly but that, if it is correctly anticipated, time is saved in the subsequent response-selection stage, because the selection is done ahead of time. Notice that this account of the stimulus probability and repetition effects supposes a stimulus identification stage. The only argument is whether stimulus probability affects the time required for identification or the time required for retrieval of the response.

One approach to the problem of choosing between the two possibilities is to vary the compatibility of the response assignment. If stimulus probability influences only stimulus identification, then high probability events should enjoy the same advantage over low probability events sharing the same response regardless of S-R compatibility. On the other hand, if stimulus probability influences response selection, more probable stimuli should have much faster RTs than less probable stimuli only when S-R compatibility is poor. Recently, Sanders (1970) confirmed this latter prediction. He assigned two letters to one verbal response and two other letters to another verbal response. The response for one of the letters in each pair was compatible because it involved the name of the letter. The same response was incompatible for the other letter in the pair. As expected, the RT was much faster for the letter that had a high probability of occurrence, but only when the S-R relationship was also incompatible. This supports the contention that stimulus probability affects primarily the memory retrieval stage rather than the stimulus identification stage.

Stimulus Similarity

When several stimuli, each requiring a different response, are similar to each other, RT to the stimuli increases.

(See Crossman 1955 and Woodworth 1938 for reviews.) This has suggested to some theorists that increased similarity prolongs the time required to identify stimuli, not the time required to select a response. That conclusion is not necessarily warranted. Morton's logogen model again allows an alternate explanation. As noted before, the logogen model assumes that a stimulus results in the accumulation of information not only in the associated response logogen but also in other logogens. The more similar are two stimuli, the more they influence the logogens of each other. Or, to phrase the notion another way, when one stimulus is similar to another, there is a tendency to emit the response appropriate to one stimulus in the presence of the other. To maintain a low error rate when there are similar stimuli, one must accumulate more information in the response logogens and hence increase RT.

One way to determine whether stimulus similarity affects the response selection stage is to determine whether the detrimental effects of increased stimulus similarity are compounded when there are incompatible S-R relationships. Rabbitt (1967) found that differences in stimulus discriminability were magnified when the relationship between lights and keys was made incompatible. This finding supports the view that stimulus similarity affects the accumulation of information in a response logogen. Other studies (such as that of Biederman and Kaplan 1970), however, found increased stimulus similarity to increase RT nearly the same amount for compatible S-R arrangements as for incompatible arrangements. This does not necessarily mean that stimulus similarity does not influence response selection; it does mean that there is as yet no clear-cut evidence suggesting that stimulus similarity affects only stimulus identification or only response selection.

Although the distinction between stimulus identification and response selection may be useful for some purposes, it is not necessarily true that all effects of stimulus variables are attributable to the identification stage. A more fruitful approach than distinguishing between stimulus identification and response selection might be to consider that several sorts of information can be stored in memory concerning a stimulus. The information may include a name for the stimulus as well as information regarding the appropriate response. When there has been little practice on the response, the name may well mediate between the stimulus and the response, although such mediation is not logically necessary. In that sense, identification may precede response selection. At more advanced stages of practice, however, the response information may be activated as early as the name. Posner (1970) found, for example, that letters can be identified as letters as rapidly as they can be identified by name. For the experienced typist, the appropriate key press in response to a letter may become available independently of the name. The distinction between stimulus identification and response selection may not then be useful.

Memory Retrieval and Attention

People are continually bombarded by many signals—sounds, sights, smells, kinesthetic sensations, vestibular sensations, and so on. Some of the signals can be ignored, but others cannot, and simultaneous or near-simultaneous decisions about appropriate action must be made. It is clear from the preceding that such decisions take time, but it is not necessarily the case that they also take attention. They may or may not interfere with each other. Organizing information for storage in LTM has been shown to require attention. What about retrieving information? Does the process of ignoring some information demand attention?

Gating Out Information

Suppose that two or more sources of information are presented, but some information is irrelevant for determining the response and hence can be ignored or "gated out." Does the gating of irrelevant information affect RT to the relevant information? Subjects in a study by Archer (1954) were to press a lever up or down, depending on the value of a single relevant dimension, such as the shape of a stimulus. In the control case, the stimuli varied only on the relevant dimension. In another case, however, the stimuli also varied on a second dimension, such as size, which had no bearing on the proper response. A third case involved two irrelevant dimensions, such as size and color. The times required to classify thirty-two stimuli successively by pressing levers were 2.24, 2.12, and 2.34 minutes with zero, one, or two irrelevant dimensions, respectively. Thus, the presence of irrelevant information made essentially no difference in RT to relevant information.

Other studies have also shown no detrimental effect of irrelevant information. This is indeed fortunate. Since people are limited in their ability to deal simultaneously with many signals, it is very useful that they can ignore some of the signals and still respond efficiently to the relevant material. In some cases, however, irrelevant information does interfere with the processing of relevant information. Morgan and Alluisi (1967) and Well (1971) found that, when the relevant dimension is hard to discriminate, then irrelevant information interferes. In addition, when the irrelevant information indicates a response that conflicts with the correct response, interference occurs. More will be said about this latter source of interference when the Stroop effect is discussed.

Psychological Refractory Period

Although much of the vast overload of information presented to the senses is gated out, often with no interference effect, many situations require that two or more sources of information each be responded to. A large number of studies have examined the processing of nearly simultaneous signals, and the major findings are very clear; people are indeed limited in completely processing more than one signal at a time. (See Smith 1967 for an excellent review of the literature.)

Typically, a signal such as a color is presented, and a rapid response such as a key press is required. At some time before the subject responds to the first signal, a second signal such as a tone is presented, requiring a second response. When RT to the second signal (RT_2) is compared to the RT to the same signal in isolation, it is almost always found that, in the two-signal situation, RT_2 is considerably increased. The delay in RT_2 is usually about equal to the time that elapses between the onset of the second signal and the execution of the first response. It is as though the subject is refractory to the second signal until the first signal is completely processed. Hence the period of interference is called the *psychological refractory period*, or PRP. Usually, RT to the first signal is unaffected by the occurrence of the second, but this is not always the case. Gottsdanker, Broadbent, and Van Sant (1963), for example, found some delays in response to the first signal when a second signal occurred soon after the first. Figure 21 illustrates the time sequence of events in the psychological refractory period.

The PRP phenomenon is very general and occurs even when the two signals are in different sensory modalities and when two different response systems are used. The limitation is therefore central and not sensory or motor. For this reason, the PRP is called an attentional limitation. Even with extended practice, the interference typically does not disappear. Gottsdanker and Stelmach (1971) trained a subject for 129 sessions in responding to

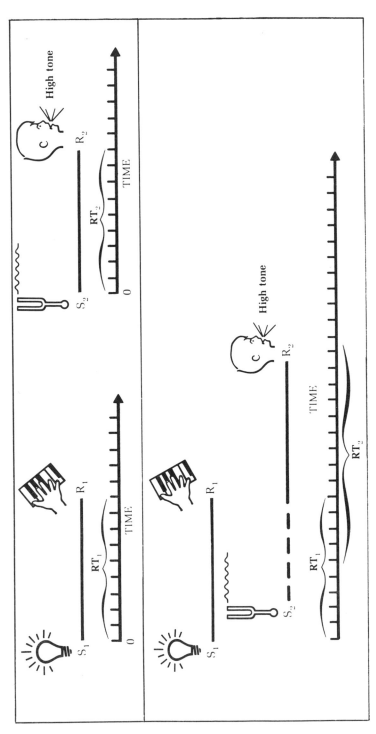

Figure 21. The top panel illustrates RT to two different signals isolated from each other in time. The lower panel illustrates the delay in processing one signal when it is presented during the processing time of another signal.

two successive visual signals. Although the magnitude of the PRP effect was reduced, it did not disappear. In almost all cases people are unable to process completely two signals, each requiring a different response, without interference. Practically the only time that the PRP does not occur is a situation in which the person knows in advance exactly what stimulus will occur and exactly when it will occur, and when he has had considerable practice (see Reynolds 1966).

The Source of Limitation

When two nearly simultaneous sources of information are both processed to the point of yielding separate responses, there is interference. The organism is clearly limited somewhere in the processing sequence. What is the source of the limitation? The answer to this question has much to say about the nature of attention.

To refine the question, it is useful to conceptualize two general processing stages—memory retrieval, and subsequent operations. The first stage involves the connecting of input information to knowledge stored in memory. Such knowledge may concern an appropriate response, or the meaning of a word, or the correct pronunciation of a word. Morton's logogen model has been used to describe the stage in which information stored in memory becomes activated. When information has accumulated to a sufficient degree in a logogen, then a second stage of operating upon one source of information can proceed. Earlier, it was suggested that rehearsal of a word, the process of practicing it in a new context, is a mental operation. For the RT situation, the operation subsequent to retrieval might be called *response initiation*.

It is possible to make finer subdivisions. As mentioned earlier, some theorists have divided the memory retrieval stage into the stimulus identification and the response selection substages. The response initiation phase could likewise be divided into the operation of initiating a movement and the actual execution of the movement. But, for present purposes, the two-stage analysis is sufficient.

The question of interest is now whether the memory retrieval stage or the response initiation stage is the source of limitation in processing nearly simultaneous signals. Can two inputs simultaneously activate appropriate information stored in memory, or must they contact memory successively? Can two responses be initiated simultaneously without interference, or does conflict occur in that stage?

Stroop effect. One method for investigating the locus of interference utilizes the gating phenomenon discussed earlier. It is possible that irrelevant information is not processed—that it does not contact memory. It is also possible that the irrelevant stimulation does elicit information stored memory at the same time as the relevant stimulation elicits relevant information, but still it does not interfere.

In a study by Keele (1972), subjects were to respond to the ink colors, red, green, yellow, and blue, by pressing four keys. In one case, the colors were printed in irrelevant forms, such as $\bowtie \pm \sqrt{}$. When compared to a control case in which form did not vary, the irrelevant information caused no increase in RT to the relevant color. In a third case, the irrelevant forms were letters, and the letters spelled out a conflicting color; for example, *green* was printed in red ink. In this case, the irrelevant forms did interfere with the RT to the color of ink. This result is the well-known Stroop effect. The critical condition in Keele's study involved a fourth type of irrelevant form. Again, subjects were to respond to the color of ink, and again the irrelevant forms spelled words, but the irrelevant words were noncolor words, such as *bird.* In this case, the presence of the word forms did not interfere with response to color.

Thus, it appears that irrelevant information, even though it *may* not cause interference, does contact memory at the same time as the relevant information. If the irrelevant information had not contacted memory, color words could not have caused interference. A discrimination of word meaning can only be made on the basis of meaning stored in memory. Recently, Hintzman and others (1972) extended the study of the Stroop effect to include a condition in which the color of ink and the word form coincided on some trials; for example, *red* was printed in red ink. RT in those cases was faster than normal, indicating again that the irrelevant word contacts information in memory without interfering with the processing of relevant information. Thus, it is not the retrieval stage per se that is limited. Instead, the product that is retrieved may cause conflict and increase RT if the color of ink suggests one response but the name of the color suggests a different response. When the irrelevant information is either a congruent color word or a neutral (noncolor) word, retrieval occurs without yielding conflicting responses.

Karlin and Kestenbaum experiment. The Stroop effect suggests that memory retrieval is not the bottleneck in information processing. The implication is that the subsequent stage of response initiation is the source of limitation. Supporting evidence for this hypothesis comes from a study by Karlin and Kestenbaum (1968), who found not only that *memory retrieval does not appear to require attention,* but also that *the time for memory retrieval can be increased and retrieval remains non-attentive.*

Before describing this complex study, it may be useful to develop an analogy in which retrieving a library book corresponds to memory retrieval, and checking out the book corresponds to response initiation. Imagine that a librarian requires ten minutes to locate book A, five minutes to locate book B, and eight minutes to locate book C (it is important that the location of A take longer than either B or C). The time required to check out a book is one minute.

Consider two cases. In one case, book B is requested immediately after book A. In the other case, book C, which takes three minutes longer to find than book B, is requested immediately after book A. How long will it take to check out book B? How long to check out book C? The answer depends on the number of librarians.

When only one librarian is available, only one book can be retrieved at a time. This is analogous to saying that only one stimulus can contact memory at a time. To check out book B, it first takes the librarian ten minutes to find A, then five minutes to find B. (It is assumed that during retrieval of B, A can be checked out.) Finally, one minute is needed to check out book B, for a total of sixteen minutes to process the book. When book C is requested after book A, it takes ten minutes for A plus eight minutes for C plus one minute to check out C, or nineteen minutes total. Book C takes precisely three minutes longer to process than book B, which is also the amount by which they differ in retrieval time. In other words, with a limitation of only one librarian, book C always takes longer than book B because its retrieval time is longer.

Now imagine that there is more than one librarian, which is analogous to saying that two or more sources of information can contact memory simultaneously. Book B is requested immediately after book A. It takes one librarian ten minutes to find A. By that time, B has already been found by another librarian, but it cannot be checked out until A has been processed, since A was requested first. One minute is then spent to check out book A plus one minute to check out book B, for a total of twelve minutes to process book B. In the case of book C, it takes ten minutes to find A plus one minute to check out A plus one minute to check out C, or twelve minutes total. With two librarians, when either B or C is preceded by A, it takes the same amount of time—twelve minutes—to complete the processing, despite the fact that retrieval time is longer for C than for B. There is ample time to retrieve either B or C while A is being retrieved, but neither B nor C can be checked out until A has been processed.

The study by Karlin and Kestenbaum is similar in principle to this library analogy. The procedure and results are shown in figure 22. One signal consisted of two possible digits presented

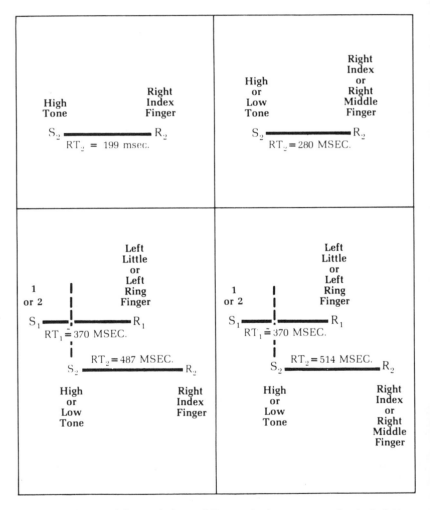

Figure 22. The top left panel shows RT to a single tone occurring in isolation. The lower left panel shows RT to the same tone when it follows another signal by 90 milliseconds. The top right panel illustrates the increase in RT when the number of possible tones is increased to two. The lower right panel illustrates RT to one of the two tones when it follows the other signal. (Based on Karlin and Kestenbaum, 1968)

visually and responded to by pressing buttons with one of two fingers on the left hand. The RT to the visual signal was approximately 370 milliseconds. Another signal consisted, in one case, of a single tone, and in another case, it consisted of one of two possible tones. In both cases, the desired response to the tone was a button press with a finger on the right hand. The one-tone case had an RT of 199 milliseconds, and the two-tone case had an RT of 280 milliseconds. Memory retrieval time is increased by 81 milliseconds when choice is added.

In the critical condition of the Karlin and Kestenbaum study, a tone was presented 90 milliseconds after a digit. The one-librarian model predicts a difference of 81 milliseconds between the one-tone and two-tone conditions; the model using two or more librarians predicts no difference between the two conditions. The basis of the latter prediction is this: while the digit is being processed, the response to the following tone also is being retrieved. But because two independent responses may not be initiated without interference, the second response must be delayed until some time following the first response, even though the second response has been retrieved. The delay in responding to the tone is not because memory retrieval has not occurred but because the second response must wait on the first response.

The results showed RT to the second signal to be 487 milliseconds in the one-tone situation and 514 milliseconds in the two-tone case. The difference between the two conditions is only 27 milliseconds, considerably less than the 81 milliseconds predicted if only one signal were able to contact memory at a time. It appears, therefore, that while the first signal is being processed, the second signal is also able to contact memory. However, the difference in RTs is 27 milliseconds and not 0 milliseconds, as predicted by the two-librarian model. This may perhaps be explained by the fact that RT to the digit is so short that in some cases memory retrieval for the subsequent tone is not completed by the time the digit is responded to. The delay in responding to the second signal depends primarily not on the difficulty of the second signal but on an inability to initiate a new response during or shortly after initiating a prior response. Psychological refractoriness therefore appears to be not in the retrieval stage but in the subsequent operations stage.

In view of the importance of this finding, it is useful to restate it in a slightly different way. The attention demands of task components are determined by the degree of interference among the tasks. When the first of two signals takes a relatively long time to process, the difficulty of the second signal can be manipulated by increasing the number of possible alternatives and, consequently, the processing time. But increased processing time causes little change in the degree of interference between the two signals. Consequently, we conclude that whatever component requiring the additional time does not require attention. When processing difficulty increases, the time required to retrieve from memory information concerning the appropriate response increases. Thus, it appears that memory retrieval does not demand attention, even though the complexity of the retrieval process, as measured in time required for processing, can be manipulated.

Confirmatory evidence. When gating occurs, there is only one response to a single stimulus presentation. The irrelevant information, although it may contact memory, does not interfere unless it leads to a conflicting response or unless the relevant information is difficult to process. When additional information is not irrelevant but instead requires a separate response, interference occurs, and such interference is called the PRP. Karlin and Kestenbaum's work indicates that the interference arises in the response initiation stage, not in the retrieval stage. At about the same time as the Karlin and Kestenbaum study, Schvaneveldt (1969) came to the same conclusion. He presented two signals simultaneously, one requiring a verbal response and the other a manual response. The complexities of the two decisions were manipulated by varying both the number of possible alternate signals and the compatibility of the S-R relationships. Exact quantitative predictions are difficult in the Schvaneveldt experiment because it did not specify which signal should be responded to first. Nevertheless, it is clear that, although increases in the complexity of one signal led to increased RT, the increased complexity did not increase the interference with processing of the other signal as much as would be expected were memory retrieval limited. Complexity was measured by the time required to process a signal, manipulated by S-R compatibility as well as by number of alternatives, and is not the same as complexity measured by attention demands.

Morton (1969*b*) required subjects to sort cards into six piles. In one case, the sorting was based on the digit that appeared on each card, with digits ranging from 1 to 6. In a second case, the sorting was based on the number of x marks, ranging from one to six, that appeared on each card. In a third case, the number of digits on a card and the value of the digits were redundant (for example, 1, 22, 333, 4444, and so on). Morton found that the third case, with two, redundant sources of information and a single response, resulted in faster sorting than the cases in which there was a single stimulus cue. His data are best explained by supposing that when redundant information is presented, both sources of information simultaneously contact memory, and hence there is no interference. Since, in addition, the two sources indicate the same response, response facilitation might be expected.

A number of other studies have shown that the processing of multiple sources of relevant information involves no interference when the final output is a single response. This lack of interference appears both when the multiple sources are redundant, as in Morton's study (see also Biederman and Checkosky 1970; and Garner and Felfoldy 1970), and when they are not redundant. Hawkins (1969), for example, showed that when subjects were to judge whether two stimuli were the same or different, the RT to make a "same" judgment was independent of whether the judgment was based on three dimensions (color, form, and size) or only on one dimension (size).

Using a different approach, Keele (1970) presented subjects with stimuli composed of one of two colors and one of two forms. In one case, a certain color-form combination required a single response. For example, a red plus symbol required a particular key press and a green 5 required a different key press. Since there were four stimulus combinations, there were four responses. In a second case, the subject responded to the color component by pressing a key with a finger on one hand and to the form component by pressing a key with a finger on the other hand. Thus, each signal required two responses, one for each component. Although the same stimulus information was processed in both conditions, the second condition, requiring two responses for each stimulus, resulted in considerably longer RTs, as would be expected if there is a limitation in initiating independent responses.

Many experiments, therefore, lead to a consistent conclusion. When more than one source of information is processed, the sources can contact memory simultaneously and without interference. But if the results of memory retrieval lead to different responses, then there is interference. Only one operation of response initiation can be performed at a time.

Some puzzling results. Although many studies indicate that memory retrieval does not take attention while response initiation does, there are a few discrepant results. Keele (1967) varied the RT of button-tapping in response to lights by changing the compatibility of the S-R relationships. In a second task, the subjects counted backward by ones, threes, or sevens from a three-digit number presented at the beginning of a trial. When the two tasks were performed together, tasks with long RTs interfered considerably more with each other than did tasks with short RTs. A detailed look at the results showed them to be in direct contradiction with the Karlin and Kestenbaum and the Schvaneveldt findings. Perhaps one reason for the discrepancy is that, in Keele's study, subjects had very little practice on extremely difficult tasks; each subject participated in only one experimental session. The studies by Karlin and Kestenbaum and by Schvaneveldt utilized more extensive practice on generally easier tasks.

At the other extreme, Seibel (1963) gave subjects over two hundred sessions of practice on key-pressing in response to simultaneously presented lights. There were ten lights, each of which might or might not be illuminated on a particular trial, and ten response keys corresponding to the lights. After the practice period, Seibel found that all the lights on a given trial could be responded to, on the average, in only 350 milliseconds, which is very fast. An inability to initiate independent responses without interference appears to have been overcome by extensive practice.

There are several aspects of both the Keele and the Seibel studies that are quite different from other studies of attention, and it is highly speculative to suppose that, with little practice, memory retrieval and response initiation both require attention, while with a great deal of practice, neither stage is attention-demanding. In the Seibel study, all signals occurred simultaneously, and all responses were made simultaneously. It may be this special feature that resulted in a lack of interference between signals. As reported earlier, Gottsdanker and Stelmach (1971) found interference between the processing of two signals to persist even with a great deal of practice, when signals and responses were not simultaneous. A complete understanding of the relationship of attention to RT is yet to be obtained.

The logogen model and multiple inputs.   Earlier, Morton's logogen model was discussed with reference to the effects of information, compatibility, and practice on RT. It was suggested that for each possible response, there is a corresponding logogen; when a signal occurs, *all* the logogens for the response set in question simultaneously accumulate information. The response is determined by the accumulation of a critical amount of information in one logogen. Such a model is congruent with the notion that, when there is more than one input, several different signals may contact memory simultaneously.

Many of the results of multiple-input experiments are understandable by assuming not only that all the logogens associated with one signal accumulate information simultaneously, but that the logogens corresponding to different signals also become activated simultaneously. The result may be that one logogen in each set reaches its activation criterion level at about the same time. Even though sufficient information may have accrued for separate responses, apparently only one such source of memory information can then be operated on at a time.

When the same logogen is common to two or more sources of information, as in Morton's study of redundant information, the logogen should build up information faster, leading to a reduced RT. This is, of course, exactly what Morton found. When one source of information is irrelevant, it typically has no effect, because the logogens activated by it are not included in the set leading to the relevant responses. But when the irrelevant information activates a conflicting logogen in the response set under consideration (the Stroop effect), the criterion of activation must be adjusted, resulting in longer RTs.

Summary

When a signal occurs and a rapid decision is made concerning action, the decision time is measured by reaction time (RT) techniques. A large number of variables affect the time required to make a decision, several of which are summarized in the Hick-Hyman law: $RT = a + bH_T$. This simple statement relating RT to information summarizes the effects of number of alternatives, probability of various alternatives, sequential dependencies, and speed-accuracy trade-off.

It might be hoped that the Hick-Hyman law could predict the decision time for a particular amount of information. Unfortunately, the constant b in the Hick-Hyman law is only constant within certain limits. With different relationships between stimuli and responses and with differing amounts of practice, the value of b changes, in some cases approaching zero. In almost all cases, however, the relationship between RT and information remains linear. And in no case does choice RT fall below about 200 to 250 milliseconds.

The model best in accord with the various RT phenomena is Morton's logogen model, which is essentially a response-conflict notion. One phenomenon the logogen model does not explicitly treat, however, is the repetition effect. The RT to a repeated event is considerably faster than that to an event that last occurred a while ago. A number of studies have led to the conclusion that the repetition effect involves a short-circuiting of the normal memory retrieval stage to which the logogen model is applicable. The advantage of repetition seems primarily attributable to the effect of checking to determine whether the stimulus is the same as the preceding one; if so, the same response can be produced as previously. If some other event is anticipated, response to that event is facilitated, and repetitions are responded to little faster than nonrepeated events. Some stimulus probability effects also seem attributable to a bypassing of memory retrieval.

Usually, however, people are faced not with a single stimulus requiring a single response, but with a barrage of stimulation—sights, sounds, smells, tastes, and kinesthetic sensations. Most of the stimulation is gated out, with few adverse effects on the processing of relevant information. But people are clearly limited in their ability to make more than one decision at the same time. Evidence from a number of studies indicates that the source of limitation is not the activation of units in memory, but the subsequent stage of operating on the retrieved information by initiating a response. Since the definition of attention is based on interference, it is concluded that memory retrieval does not take attention, while response initiation does.

Perhaps the most interesting conclusion about the nature of attention concerns the fact that memory retrieval can be considerably increased in difficulty, as measured by time required to process a signal. Difficulty can be increased by varying the amount of information and by varying the S-R compatibility. Such increased difficulty has no effect on attention.

Occasionally, you may try to recover information from memory and fail, yet you are sure that you know the answer. The name of an acquaintance, for example, may temporarily slip your mind. After failing to remember, you may go about other tasks, and suddenly, perhaps an hour later or even a week later, the answer may pop into your mind, even though you are doing some other task at the time. Is this a case in which memory retrieval takes an inordinately long time yet still requires no attention?

At this point, one may wonder whether retrieval of information from memory ever requires attention. To say no would undoubtedly be wrong. Retrieval is not always direct. Attempts to recall some information may require an active search process. An attempt may be made to reconstruct the context of the original learning and to recall the information from the context. Partial information may be recalled, and the memory search may be redirected from the partial information. Surely, such a complicated retrieval process requires attention. But complicated retrieval processes may be viewed as compounds of several substages of retrieval and mental operations. The mental operations of comparing, evaluating, and redirecting the retrieval process may be attention-demanding, while the actual retrieval substage is not. These problems of retrieval and mental operations will be further developed in chapter 7.

 Chapter 6

MOVEMENT CONTROL

In the process of adapting to the environment, man stores information in memory and later retrieves it. Adaptation is not complete, however, until there is a movement in response to the information. (Glandular responses also constitute adaptation, but they are not considered here.) Indeed, some have claimed that the brain exists ultimately only to control movement. With the advent of machines, man's strength was greatly amplified, but very precise and complex movements were often required to control the machines. As automation has progressed, many of the skilled movements formerly required have been replaced by simpler movements, and machines now perform increasingly complex series of movements autonomously. Nevertheless, a major part of people's lives is still spent in direct interaction with their environments, and such interaction requires skilled movement control.

Sometimes, the movement is simply the displacement of a limb to a target, perhaps followed by a grasping or releasing movement. Other cases involve a series of movements such as those involved in walking or speaking. A series of movements can be viewed simply as a string of individual movements, each directed to a separate target. This may be an accurate description of movement control early in the development of some skills, but considerable evidence indicates that the control of a well-practiced series of movements is quite different than the control of a single, precise movement directed to a target. Consequently, single movements and series of movements will be considered separately here.

Fitts's Law

Movement time (MT) is measured from the beginning until the end of the actual movement. It excludes reaction time (RT), which is measured from the onset of the stimulus to the onset of the movement. Answers to the deceptively simple question of how much time a movement requires have been quite contradictory. On the one hand, Brown and Slater-Hammel (1949) showed that the time required to move from a starting point and hit a narrow line increased as the distance to the line increased. Furthermore, the increase in MT was a logarithmic function of distance. Adding one inch to a ten-inch movement, for example, has little effect on MT; adding one inch to a one-inch movement has quite a large effect. The findings of Brown and Slater-Hammel seem commonsensical.

It is easy, however, to demonstrate situations in which MT does not depend on distance. One can write a word on a blackboard in practically the same amount of time that it takes to write it in small letters on a piece of paper, despite the fact that the total distance moved on the blackboard is perhaps two or three hundred times as great as that moved on paper! Similarly, one can tap a finger nearly as fast at medium amplitudes as with very short strokes. One can move an arm back and forth equally rapidly with relatively long or short excursions.

Fitts (1954) was perhaps the first psychologist to state explicitly that MT depends on movement precision as well as on movement distance. Basic writing strokes on a blackboard are not only very long, they also deviate in length from one instance to another. The upward stroke in the letter t may differ by a half-inch on successive repetitions with little loss in readability. A similar deviation in the size of small letters on a piece of paper would make them completely unreadable, since the letters may average only one-eighth inch in height. It is necessary, therefore, to control the accuracy of movement as well as the distance moved in attempting to specify MT.

Fitts (1954) and Fitts and Peterson (1964) systematically varied movement distance and width of target. In the latter study, subjects quickly moved a stylus held in the hand from a starting position to a target either three, six, or twelve inches away. The target width was one-eighth, one-quarter, one-half, or one inch. MT increased from about 140 milliseconds at the shortest distance and widest target to about 500 milliseconds at the longest distance and narrowest target. In general, MT is given by the following equation, now referred to as Fitts's law:

$MT = a + (b \log_2 2D/W)$, where a and b are constants, D is the distance from the starting position to the target center, and W is the target width. In the Fitts and Peterson experiment, the constant a was -70 milliseconds, and b was $+74$ milliseconds, averaged over several subjects. From those values, MT of the hand and arm for any combination of target distance and precision can be predicted quite well.

There are two important features of Fitts's law. First, if the distance is increased while width is held constant, or if the width is decreased while distance is held constant, MT increases. Furthermore, the increase is logarithmic. Each time the distance is doubled, the MT increases a constant amount; each time the width is halved, the MT increases a constant amount.

The second and perhaps more interesting point is that proportional changes in width and distance exactly compensate for each other; if distance is doubled and so is target width, there is no change in MT. This simple law resolves the dilemma posed by the handwriting example and by the Brown and Slater-Hammel data. Since subjects in the Brown and Slater-Hammel experiment were required to terminate the movement on a narrow line, the target width may be considered to be constant, while the movement distance varied. Consequently, MT increased. For the handwriting example, in contrast, the *relative* accuracy remains approximately constant with different stroke sizes; as the average length of a stroke increases, the average amount by which a stroke deviates from the average stroke length also increases. Since the ratio of stroke length to stroke accuracy is approximately constant, MT does not change.

Fitts and Peterson discovered that the variables that influence MT differ from those that affect RT. RT is virtually unaffected by the precision and distance of the ensuing movement. In contrast, RT is considerably decreased by increased probability of signals designating the desired movement; this has only a small effect on MT. The decision regarding where to move and the control of the actual movement appear to be quite independent.

Feedback and Fitts's Law

Given that Fitts's law describes MT very well, we are left with the problem of deciding which processes determine the function. One possibility is that, in moving his hand toward a target, a person can see when he is missing the target and make appropriate corrections. The farther the distance and the narrower the target, the more corrections are needed. If each correction takes an approximately equal time, then MT is simply equal to some time, *t*, the time required to process visual feedback and correct the movement, multiplied by the number of corrections, *n*.

One problem with this feedback analysis of Fitts's law is that earlier work by Woodworth (1899) and by Vince (1948) indicates that it takes about 500 milliseconds to correct a movement. This is much too long to account for the rapid adjustments that would be needed to explain Fitts's results, in which the longest movement was only 500 milliseconds. Perhaps the time required to process visual feedback as estimated by Vince and Woodworth is too long.

Time required to process visual feedback. To determine how long it takes to process visual feedback, Keele and Posner (1968) required subjects to move a stylus a distance of six inches to a target one-quarter inch in diameter. The subjects were trained to complete the movement in 150, 250, 350, and 450 milliseconds. (The average measured MTs were about 190, 260, 350, and 440 milliseconds.) Of course, the faster the movement, the more often the target was missed. On some trials, all lights were turned off as soon as the movement began, so the movement was completed in the dark. The results were that movements of 190 milliseconds were performed with equal accuracy whether the light remained on or not. Movements of 260 milliseconds or slower, however, missed the target fewer times when the lights stayed on during movement. It was concluded, therefore, that it takes approximately 190 to 260 milliseconds for visual feedback to be useful for movement correction.

The finding that movements can be corrected in a much shorter time than previously thought suggests that a movement lasting 500 milliseconds, such as the twelve-inch movement to a one-eighth inch target in the Fitts and Peterson study, can actually be composed of an initial motion toward the target and two or three corrections, on the average. Can the function found by Fitts be derived from feedback considerations? Crossman and Goodeve (1963) and Keele (1968) demonstrated that it can. Two assumptions are necessary. One assumption is that each correction takes an approximately equal amount of time. Keele and Posner estimated that amount of time to be between 190 and 260 milliseconds. Second, it must be assumed that the relative accuracy of each submovement is constant—that is, the average distance by which a movement misses the center of the target divided by the distance of the movement is about the same for all lengths of movement. Vince (1948) estimated the value of this constant to be about 7 percent. For instance, a movement of ten inches will miss the center of the target by about 0.7 inches, on the average. A movement of one inch will miss the target center by about 0.07 inches, on the average. The two assumptions can be shown (see Keele 1968) to lead to the same logarithmic function proposed by Fitts. Furthermore, the constants for time required to process visual feedback and for the relative accuracy of sub-movement predict quite well the actual MTs found by Fitts and Peterson.

Attention demands of single movements.   The view that precise movements consist of a series of movements corrected by feedback processing suggests that movement control consists of a series of decisions not unlike those discussed in the preceding chapter. The signal requiring a response is the discrepancy between the predicted termination point of the moving limb and the position of the target; the response to the discrepancy is the movement correction. If movements involve a series of decisions, then they should also require attention. Just as people are refractory to processing signals, at least as far as response initiation goes, they may also be at least partially refractory to processing a signal while engaged in a precise movement requiring corrections.

To determine whether such movements require attention, Posner (see Posner and Keele 1969) had subjects align a pointer with either a narrow or a wide target by turning a knob. At various points during the movement, a noise signal occurred to which the subjects responded simply by pressing a key with their free hand. The increase in RT to the signal was a measure of the attention demand of the movement task. In a control condition, no movement was required, but subjects responded to the noise signal. When compared to the control, the experimental RT was increased at all points during the movement, particularly as the target was approached. In addition, the RT was always greater during movement to the narrow target than during movement to the wide target. Precise movements may therefore be said to require attention, the greater the movement precision, the more attention required. The results of Posner's study are just as would be expected if a total movement were composed of a number of corrected movements. More corrections would tend to occur near the target, resulting in increased attention demands at that range. More corrections would be required for narrower than for wider targets; narrower targets would require more attention.

The implication so far has been that movement per se does not require attention; rather, movement corrections do. A movement involving no correction should not interfere with a probe signal. Posner confirmed this prediction; movements stopped by a peg did not interfere with RT to a noise signal that occurred during the movement. In other words, movements that do not need visual monitoring and correction require no attention.

More recently, Ells (1969) systematically analyzed attention demands during the period preceding a movement, while the decision regarding movement target is being made, and during the actual movement itself. As Posner did, Ells introduced a probe signal (in this case a tone) at various points following a signal designating the movement target and at various points during the actual movement. His findings replicated most of the important features of earlier work. RTs to signals introduced during the decision period preceding actual movement were increased, as in typical psychological refractory period experiments. RTs to signals introduced during the actual movement depended on the accuracy of the movement, with narrow targets requiring more attention than wide targets, and movement to a stop requiring no attention at all. In addition, Ells found that the attention demand during the decision period did not depend on the difficulty of the ensuing movement. Furthermore, the attention demand during movement depended solely on the precision of the movement and not on the difficulty of the preceding decision regarding the movement target. As in the Fitts and Peterson study, the decision of where to move and movement control itself appear to be independent of each other.

In the last chapter, the psychological refractory period was discussed; it has been found that, while a person is reacting to one signal, his response to a second signal is delayed. Further analysis led to the conclusion that the response initiation component of RT requires attention, but the memory retrieval component does not. A similar analysis of MT is desirable. Since movements to a mechanical stop are not dependent on visual feedback and do not require attention, it is inferred that movement per se does not require attention, but the corrective process does. The corrective process actually involves two parts. First, visual feedback must be monitored. More precisely, the termination point of the movement, predicted from the speed and position of the moving limb, must be compared with the position of the target. Second, when an error is detected, a correction must be initiated. Does the monitoring of visual feedback require attention? Or, as in the case of RT, is it the actual initiation of a correction that requires attention?

Feedback and the recalibration of movements. The ability to hit a narrow target requires that visual input which indicates that the target will be missed be translated into appropriate corrective movements. The ability of human beings to utilize visual feedback in making appropriate movement corrections is not well developed at birth. Babies have a very difficult time reaching for objects, presumably because they have not yet acquired such an ability. In fact, Bruner (1968) found that seven-month-old infants sometimes close their eyes when reaching for an object, as if visual feedback would actually interfere with movement control once movement had begun! Other times, infants seem to block out visual feedback by not focusing on the object they are reaching for. The relationship between feedback and movements is learned over a long period of time. Many animals require some learning to calibrate feedback with movements. Hailman (1969), for example, found that the pecking accuracy of gull chicks improves in the first few days after hatching. That this improvement is due to learning and not to maturation was shown by delaying the pecking experiences of some chicks and finding that improvement still occurred with practice.

Adult humans, however, can observe the positions of hand and target and initiate a corrective hand movement with about 7 percent accuracy. That is, the average distance of a hand-held pointer from the target center following a single corrective motion is about 7 percent of the distance moved (Vince 1948). But suppose the relationship between visual feedback and movement is artificially changed. After a lifetime of learning the relationship between vision and movement, how long does it take a person to make a readjustment when his vision is altered?

McLaughlin (1967), in an ingenious study, had subjects fix their eyes on a spot. When a light was illuminated 10 degrees to the side of the spot, they were to rapidly shift their gaze to the light. Such movements of the eye are very quick, requiring only about 40 milliseconds. Eye movements also appear to be more accurate than hand movements; in McLaughlin's study the target was missed by only about 0.3 degrees, or only 3 percent of the distance moved (as compared with the 7 percent reported by Vince for hand movements). After the initial accuracy was assessed, the situation was changed; once the subject's eye began moving,

McLaughlin moved the light from the 10-degree position to one only 9 degrees from the starting spot. Subjects were usually unaware that the change had been made, and at first, they overshot the 9-degree position and had to make a corrective movement.[1] But after about three trials, the 10-degree signal elicited a 9-degree movement. After a few more trials, McLaughlin again changed the situation so that the 10-degree signal position remained unchanged once the eye movement was underway. The subjects now undershot the target, but, again, an appropriate adjustment was made in a very short time. Thus, very little time is needed for people to adjust their motor output in response to experimentally induced changes in their visual system.

The study by McLaughlin was concerned with the flexibility that exists between the reception of a visual input and the execution of a movement intended to focus the eye on the visual signal. Much related experimentation has been concerned with the relationship between the visual system, the kinesthetic system, and the auditory system. It has been found that many adjustments of the sensory system to the motor system are made very rapidly. (See Howard and Templeton 1966 for an extensive review of the many studies done on this problem.)

The relationship between visual input and motor output is very flexible in adults. Compensatory adjustments to small changes in the relationship are made in just a few seconds. This flexibility is the more remarkable in that it follows years of experience with a constant correspondence between input and output. Such a flexibility is reasonable from an evolutionary point of view, at least for the eye-hand system. Objects of different weights require different propulsion forces to traverse the same distance. (For example, the degree of force required to hit a target with a stone depends on the weight of the stone.) It is therefore very desirable to have a flexible arrangement between feedback from the eyes and movement control of the limbs.

Controlling Series of Movements

Many skills consist of a complex, well-practiced series of movements that tend to be repeated periodically. Walking is a familiar example. The control of such a movement series seems to be quite different from the control of precise, single

---

[1]Events that occur during a rapid, saccadic movement of the eyes are often unseen. It has been speculated that material persisting in short-term visual storage may be processed during the saccade.

movements to a target. Precise movements to a target depend very heavily on visual feedback, while many series of movements do not, or at least not in the same way. It is usually not necessary to watch one's feet while walking. Even when the movements or the direct results of the movements are watched, the individual movements still do not seem to be under direct feedback control. Instead, something like the overall progress is monitored visually. One looks ahead for obstacles and makes changes in direction or timing, rather than controlling individual segments of the walking movement.

Such a shift in the role of the visual system may occur gradually as a skill is acquired. Early in practice, individual movements may be made, the outcome analyzed by the visual system, a correction initiated, feedback analyzed again, and so on. Such a skill is said to be under closed-loop control, reflecting the circular relationship between feedback and movement. But gradually, the skill may shift to an open-loop mode, in which movements, at least for some short period, may be autonomous of visual feedback.

This shift in mode of control was demonstrated in a study by Pew (1966). Subjects attempted to keep a spot of light, which could move across an oscilloscope screen, centered on a line. The spot, which was constantly in motion, was controlled by two keys activated by the index fingers. Pressing one key caused the spot to accelerate to the left; pressing the other key caused it to accelerate to the right. Thus, centering of the light required alternate tapping of the two keys. If moving pictures of the spot were taken, records such as those shown in figure 23 would be obtained. The records show the position of the dot about the center as a function of time. The two records on the top show examples of the performance of two subjects early in practice. These patterns are irregular, with the height of the peaks and the distance between peaks being quite variable and indicating irregularities in the timing of key presses. After a few weeks of practice, the patterning exhibited by Pew's subjects changed considerably. Some subjects exhibited a very rapid and regular pattern of responding, as shown in the lower record on the left, in which there was a gradual drift off target and then a single correction. Pew called such control *open-loop*, because the movement series did not appear to be under visual control, but visual feedback was engaged periodically to effect a correction. A mode of responding adopted by other subjects, called a *modulation mode*, is shown in the lower record on the right. Again, very rapid and regular movements were made, but as the subject began

EARLY PRACTICE

Subject 1  Subject 2

LATE PRACTICE

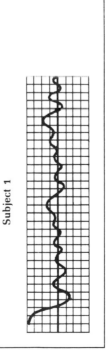 Subject 1 Subject 2

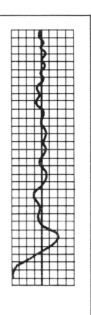

Figure 23. Position of a dot about a center position as controlled by two different operators early and later in practice. The vertical axis indicates dot position and the horizontal axis indicates time. (Revised from Pew, 1966)

to drift off target, the pattern of responding was modulated, so that one key was depressed slightly longer than the other for a series of movements. The result was a slow drift to the other side of the center line. Then the pattern was modulated again. This resulted in a slow oscillation about the center line, upon which are superimposed the regular movements. The important finding of Pew's study is that, after practice, subjects shift from visual control of individual movements to the use of visual feedback for periodic correction or modulation of the pattern of movements.

Kinesthetic control versus motor programs. If after extensive practice, the control of the individual movements involved in many skills shifts from the visual system, what is the new control mechanism? One very early theory was that successive motions in a well-practiced sequence were under kinesthetic control. According to this theory, each movement is accompanied by feedback from joint senses, muscle spindle receptors, tendon stretch receptors, and cutaneous senses. Collectively, these senses are called kinesthesis. The kinesthetic feedback from one segment of the movement pattern was seen as being instrumental in initiating the next movement in the series, and so on. Such control is referred to as *S-R chaining* (see Greenwald 1970). Basically, movement control was seen as being a series of conditioned reflexes.

The Fleishman and Rich study. For an S-R chaining mechanism to be a feasible theory of control, kinesthesis must be shown to be useful in the control of well-practiced sequences. Fleishman and Rich (1963) investigated the roles of kinesthesis and spatial orientation in learning a two-hand coordination task. A small disc moved at irregular rates around a circle. The task of a subject was to follow the disc with a spot by rotating two handles, one with each hand. One handle controlled displacement of the spot toward and away from the body and the other handle controlled right-left movements. Each subject was given forty one-minute trials on the task. In addition to the two-hand coordination task, Fleishman and Rich gave each of forty subjects two other tests. A test for kinesthetic sensitivity rated subjects on their ability to discriminate differences in weights. A spatial sensitivity test measured their ability to match pictures of views of a horizon as seen from an airplane cockpit with pictures of the orientation of a plane that would allow the corresponding view of the horizon. Subjects were then divided into the best twenty and the worst twenty on spatial sensitivity and the best twenty and the worst twenty on kinesthetic sensitivity.

The performance on the two-hand coordination task for subjects classified into high and low spatial sensitivity is shown in figure 24. Initially, subjects high on spatial sensitivity performed better on the tracking task. The reason for this is not clear; perhaps spatial sensitivity is related to the ability to utilize visual feedback and make corrective movements. With practice, both groups improved, and by the fortieth trial there was essentially no difference in performance between the two groups, suggesting that visual control becomes less important with increased practice.

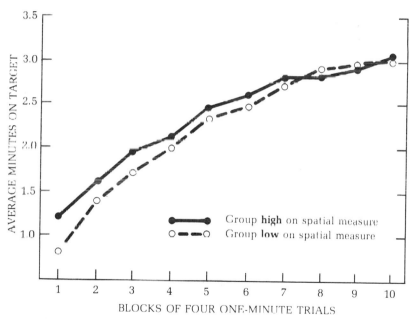

Figure 24. Time on target in a tracking task for subjects high or low in ability on a spatial task. (Revised from Fleishman and Rich, 1963)

More important is the manner in which kinesthetic sensitivity correlates with performance. These results are shown in figure 25. Initially, there was no difference in performance between subjects high on kinesthetic sensitivity and those low on kinesthetic sensitivity, but after forty practice trials on the tracking task, the group of subjects high on kinesthetic sensitivity exhibited a clear superiority in tracking. Thus, the Fleishman and Rich study leads to the conclusion that, as performance improves on skills requiring complex movements, the importance of kinesthesis increases. This is consistent with other studies that have shown better performance on tracking tasks when a variety of kinesthetic cues are available (see, for example, Notterman and Page 1962).

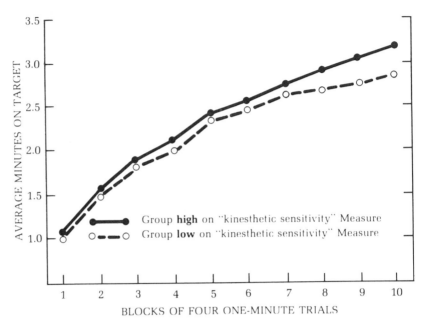

Figure 25. Subjects high or low on kinesthetic sensitivity. (Revised from Fleishman and Rich. 1963)

The Taub and Berman study. The emphasis on the role of kinesthesis in movement control comes in part from an early study by Mott and Sherrington (1895) on Rhesus monkeys. These investigators surgically eliminated feedback either from single forelimbs or from single hindlimbs of the monkeys. The sensory neurons subserving kinesthesis enter the spinal cord between the vertebrae close to the back of the spine. Consequently, it is possible to sever those nerve bundles (a process called de-afferentation) without damaging the motor neurons, which enter the spinal cord on the ventral side.

Mott and Sherrington found that animals with complete de-afferentation of one limb lost all fine movements of the limb, especially of the hands and digits. Furthermore, the limb was not used at all in walking or climbing. Instead, the animals usually walked on three legs. It was therefore felt that kinesthesis was necessary for control of skilled movements.

About sixty years after the Mott and Sherrington study, another pair of investigators, Taub and Berman (1968), repeated the earlier study and obtained similar results. A single de-afferented forelimb in a monkey was not used in skilled movements. Taub and Berman proceeded several steps further, however. They next restrained the good forelimb with a straightjacket. Instead of falling flat, the monkey now used the de-afferented limb for walking and climbing and for well-controlled grasping movements. The limb was not worthless after all, but was merely inhibited when the good limb was in use. Next, both forelimbs were de-afferented. Relatively normal use was made of both limbs in walking and climbing, even when the monkey was blindfolded. Even when all of the sensory fibers entering the spinal cord via the so-called dorsal roots were severed, so that presumably the monkey had no feeling whatsoever in its entire body, use of the forelimbs was maintained.

The Taub and Berman results, when compared to the study by Fleishman and Rich, pose a dilemma. On the one hand, kinesthesis appears to play an important role in movement skills, particularly as the skill improves. On the other hand, kinesthesis does not seem to be necessary for skilled movements. Perhaps Taub and Berman did not completely eliminate kinesthetic feedback when they severed the nerve bundles, although when they stimulated sensory nerves after de-afferentation, they found no neural responses occurring in the brain. However, Bossom and Ommaya (1968) confirmed that monkeys can execute skilled movements following de-afferentation, and they took extreme pains to insure that all kinesthetic feedback was eliminated. It appears, therefore, that skilled movements do not always require kinesthesis.

Studies with lower animals confirm this conclusion. Wilson (1961), for example, found that kinethesis is not necessary for repetitive wing beats in the locust. One should be cautious however, about generalization from locust to man. Nevertheless, some data from humans supports the same conclusion. Lazlo (1966) eliminated kinesthesis in the arms of people by temporarily cutting off the blood supply to the arm with a pressure cuff and found that regular finger-tapping could occur, despite the fact that the subjects could not feel the movements of their fingers. Lashley (1951) pointed out that successive movements often appear to be executed too quickly (in piano playing, for example) for the feedback of one movement to influence the next. Thus, there is fairly extensive evidence that movement sequences do not always require feedback for execution.

The most intriguing explanation of the dilemma posed by the Taub and Berman versus Fleishman and Rich studies is that, although kinesthetic feedback functions in skilled performance, it does not directly control the patterning of movements. Rather than functioning in an S-R chain, kinesthesis may be used in other ways.

The concept of a motor program.   If neither visual nor kinesthetic feedback is needed for the execution of patterns of movement, then the movement patterns must be represented centrally in the brain, or perhaps in some cases in the spinal cord. Such representation is called a *motor program.* As a motor program is executed, neural impulses are sent to the appropriate muscles in proper sequence, timing, and force, as predetermined by the program, and the neural impulses are largely uninfluenced by the resultant feedback.

An example of how such a program would operate can be seen by referring to figure 23. With practice, some subjects in Pew's study developed an open-loop mode of movement control. Presumably, the pattern of output to their muscles was predetermined by a motor program and executed without modification by either visual or kinesthetic feedback until error became rather gross. Other subjects developed a modulation mode of responding. Their individual movements were also presumably under motor program control, but continuous modification of the program was made on the basis of visual or kinesthetic information. The main problem in skill acquisition, at least for those skills involving predictable and regular movements, is, then, not to build up an S-R chain, but to construct a motor program.

Functions of Feedback

The Fleishman and Rich study and other studies strongly suggest that kinesthesis is important in skilled performance, but the motor program theory suggests that feedback is not used in direct control of individual movements within the sequence. Rather, the sequence is determined by central brain mechanisms. What, then are the functions of feedback from the various senses (visual, kinesthetic, auditory, and so on)? There are several potentially important functions: (1) Feedback gives information relevant to starting position. (2) Feedback is used as a program monitor. (3) Motor programs elicit gross motor patterns, but a peripheral feedback loop is used in making fine adjustments. (4) Feedback is used in the acquisition of motor programs.

Feedback on starting positions.   Before a program is begun, information regarding the position of the limbs is needed in order to determine the point in the motor program at which action should begin. The left foot cannot move forward if it already is forward. It is possible in some instances that information about limb position can come from memory of the terminal position of the preceding program, but not when a long time has elapsed since the preceding movement or the limb has been moved by external forces.

The monitoring function of feedback.   The monitoring function has already been mentioned in discussing the open-loop and modulation modes of control in Pew's study. When there is no conflict between the motor program and the actual position of the limbs (as determined by feedback), then no modification of the program is needed. But when these two sources of information do not coincide, program modification is necessary.

Consider someone who stubs his toe while walking. At the time the impediment is encountered, a set of muscle commands to place the foot in a certain position is in effect, but kinesthetic feedback (and possibly also visual, auditory, cutaneous, and vestibular feedback) indicates that the foot is in another position. Once the discrepancy is detected, a correction in the motor program must be made in order to avoid falling. If all sources of feedback were eliminated, the leg muscles could receive the proper sequence of commands, but the person could be lying on his side kicking instead of walking and not be aware of it.

Lazlo (1966) reports that when kinesthesis is eliminated by temporarily cutting off blood circulation in the arm, subjects sometimes report that their finger is not moving when in fact it is. In contrast, subjects may report that their fingers are moving when they are anesthetized and restrained. Feedback is useful, then, for monitoring the movement or position of a limb so that it can be compared with the motor program.

Many years ago, Von Holst and Mittelstaedt (see Hinde 1969 for a description of their model and others) postulated a comparison system in which the motor commands issued to muscles are accompanied by a "copy," often called corollary discharge, of the commands. The copy was said to be sent to a comparison center, and feedback from movement received by the comparison center. There, the comparison of the two sources of information is made, and corrections in the motor program are determined.[2]

Theorists have typically conceived of the comparison process as occurring in the brain. But an intriguing possibility is that some comparisons between the motor program and feedback might occur in the limb itself! How might this happen? Embedded in the muscles are kinesthetic receptors called muscle spindles. When a main muscle is stretched, the muscle spindle may be stretched, and the neural firing from the spindle increases as a consequence. If, on the other hand, the main muscle is contracted, the spindle may relax, and spindle discharge decreases. Associated with the muscle spindle is a tiny muscle called the receptor muscle that can contract or relax on its own accord and make the spindle less susceptible to stretch from the main muscle—that is, it can nullify any effect of stretch or contraction of the main muscle.

Suppose that the motor program not only sends commands to the main muscle to cause it to contract or relax, but also sends a "copy" of each command to the receptor muscle so that it mirrors the movement of the main muscle and nullifies any effect of stretch or contraction. As a result, a constant discharge would be maintained from the muscle spindle. Now imagine that the moving limb hits an unexpected impediment. The receptor muscle would continue to assume the position for which it was programmed, but the main muscle would not, since the position of the main muscle is determined by the positions of the bones in the limbs as well as by the neural commands it receives. The resulting discrepancy would cause the muscle spindle to either increase or decrease in stretch, and the neural discharge would increase or decrease correspondingly. On the basis of the discharge, an appropriate correction could be made.

At present, there appears to be no evidence that the comparison between feedback and motor program occurs in the peripheral limb, but this remains a possibility. It is possible that comparisons occur in the brain or spinal cord as well.

Feedback and fine motor adjustments. Any series of movements occurs in a changing environment. A motor program, on the other hand, is rather rigid. Presumably, however, it can be corrected or modulated from time to time, as suggested by Pew's

---

[2]The actual comparison models reviewed by Hinde were designed not to explain movement correction, but to explain how an organism can determine from an image moving across the retina whether the organism itself is moving. the environment is moving, or both. The same models apply to movement correction as well.

study. If a person were walking on a smooth, constantly level floor, with only occasional corners to turn, a rigid but slightly modifiable motor program would suffice. But on normal terrain, there are slight elevations or depressions that could throw a person off balance unless he made fine adjustments in the patterns of his feet and leg movements.

How can an organism adapt to small but unexpected changes in the environment without reverting to the inefficient, closed-loop mode of control demonstrated by Pew's subjects early in practice? One possibility, suggested by Gibbs (1970), is that a motor program sets the general patterning of a movement series, and a peripheral feedback loop makes adjustments for minor departures from the expected course of movement. The specific mechanism depends on the peripheral comparison process described for the monitoring function of feedback. Suppose that the motor program sends the normal pattern of neural impulses to the main muscles—that is, the pattern that would be issued for an unperturbed movement. A "copy" of the pattern is also sent to the corresponding receptor muscles in the spindle mechanisms. If there is no perturbation in the movement, the stretch in the main muscles and in the receptor muscles will exactly nullify each other, so there will be no change in spindle discharge. But if a slight perturbation occurs, such as a depression in the ground, then a slight discrepancy will develop between the position for which the receptor muscles are set and the degree of stretch that the main muscles achieve. The result will be either a decrease or an increase in spindle discharge, depending on whether the spindle is increased or decreased in stretch. This change in receptor neural discharge may be fed back via the spinal cord, influencing the neural impulses activating the main muscles, and boosting the neural activity sent to some muscles and reducing it in others. This process may bypass the brain altogether, or it may occur simultaneously with feedback to the brain. The result is compensatory change in the movement to adjust to the perturbation in the environment.

This system of peripheral adjustment for small departures from expected movement was developed by Gibbs on the basis of anatomical and physiological characteristics of the kinesthetic system and on the basis of some circumstantial evidence from experiments on movement control. Presumably, large discrepancies between the motor program and feedback would be handled by the brain. Although this theory is plausible and consistent with much that is known about motor control, it lacks firm evidence.

Attention demands of sequential movements. People feel that many tasks involving regular series of movements require much attention during early phases of learning. It seems likely that any skill in a closed-loop mode of control would interfere with an attention-demanding task. When single movements were discussed, it was pointed out that the processing of visual feedback and correction of movements demands attention. But as a motor program becomes better developed, longer sequences of movements should be able to be executed without corrections, and many corrections should be small enough to be handled by the peripheral feedback loop proposed by Gibbs. People feel that such movements, like pedaling a bike, require little or no attention. However, there are few formal experiments assessing interference between a repetitive task and a secondary task. Posner (1969) has shown that the regularity of moving a lever back and forth between two stops is slightly impaired by the performance of another task, but the times at which interference occurs are not known. Perhaps much of the movement is free of attention and occasional corrections are responsible for the small interference.

Although kinesthetic feedback may be continually monitored and compared with a motor program, it may not be the monitoring and comparison per se that take attention. As was proposed when discussing the attention demands of simple movements, attention may be needed only when large corrections are *issued.* Again, there are many interesting questions but few answers.

Learning of Motor Programs

Feedback, besides being useful to initiate motor programs, to monitor the progress of skills, and to make fine adjustments, is further necessary to learn motor programs. As a motor program becomes established, errors may occur in skilled performance. Feedback is needed not only to reduce the error but also to alter the program so that the same error will not be repeated. At the simplest level, crude feedback may be extrinsic to the organism (someone else may tell a person that his performance is good or bad, for example). Extrinsic feedback may also be more sophisticated (someone may tell a person, for example, not just that he missed a target, but that he moved too far). Holding (1965) has reviewed studies of the effectiveness of extrinsic feedback in acquiring skills. In this chapter, however, the role of intrinsic feedback supplied by the learner's own senses is explored.

A skilled performance has a number of consequences—kinesthetic feedback, visual effects, sounds, and so on. When those consequences match some desired result, then the correct sequence of movements has been performed. For example, the complex sequence of articulation movements involved in speaking is correct if the sound produced is the desired one. Thus, in establishing a motor program it is useful to have a model or standard of the desired output to which intrinsic feedback can be compared. If a satisfactory match is made, then the sequence can be used again with no modification. If there is a mismatch between the feedback and the model, program modification is needed. Eventually a motor program will be developed that results in the desired sequence of movements. The standard to which feedback is matched can be either external or internal (that is, stored in memory) to the learner.

External models.   An external model may be provided by simply seeing or hearing another person perform the desired movement. An attempt can then be made to copy the model, and feedback from the imitated performance can be compared with the model. There are three problems that can arise in the comparison process, however. One problem is that a permanent representation of the model may not be stored in memory. A learner must remember the model for at least short periods of time so that feedback can be compared with it. It is possible that a model is of increased value in skill learning if it is available simultaneously with imitated performance, or after such performance as well as before. This would reduce the inaccuracies of memory.

A second problem is that the feedback from a person's own senses may be considerably different than his view of the model. A person cannot see his own limbs move in the same way that he can see another person's. Similarly, a person's perception of his own voice is distorted by bone conduction and articulation. Such situations require a transformation of images. For example, a visual image of a pattern of movements might have to be translated into a kinesthetic image. One technique for avoiding inaccuracies of comparison is to record both the model's performance and the performance of the learner. For some skills, this can be done with videotape; for others, it can be done with tape recordings. Often, in language training, both the proper pronunciation and the learner's pronunciation are recorded and played back. Comparison can then be used to adjust the sequence of movements that constituted the learner's performance.

A third problem is that subjects may not be able to perceive important differences between the model and the feedback. The classic case involves learning to speak a new language. Very often, certain critical nuances of a new language are not perceived by the learner, and a variety of related sounds are perceived as being the same. No alterations can be made in incorrect pronunciation when the errors are not perceived by the learner. Kalikow (1971) as part of an experimental language program attempting to help Spanish-speaking persons learn English, has devised an ingenious approach to the speech perception problem. An oscilloscope screen is used to portray the position of the vocal apparatus (lips, tongue, and so on) necessary to produce a particular sound. When the subject produces a sound, a mathematical model is used to infer the position of the vocal apparatus that would be necessary to produce the sound, and this picture is displayed along with the model. Differences that are difficult to hear can then be seen, and attempts can be made to modify the movement sequence yielding the incorrect sound. The technique does result in improvement in pronunciation, but no comparisons have yet been made with standard teaching procedures for improving pronunciation.

Internal models. It is possible for a model of a skilled performance to be stored in memory. Such a model is called an internal model. Most studies of internal models have been concerned with bird songs, complex skills requiring a rapid series of accurate and well-timed movements. The following account is based on the fascinating reviews of bird song development by Marler and Hamilton (1966) and of Nottebohm (1970).

The songs of some bird species seem to be almost completely determined by heredity, because there is little variation within the species, and song development does not depend on prior exposure to the song. At the other extreme, some birds are very adaptable and even learn to sing tunes composed by humans (for example, the European bullfinch) or to speak words (the Indian Hill myna). More useful birds for research purposes, however, have been species such as the European chaffinch, the white-crowned sparrow, and the Oregon junco, which have a moderate degree of flexibility in song development.

Marler has shown that white-crowned sparrows raised in isolation from other sparrows shortly after hatching do not develop the normal song. If, however, the young birds are exposed to the adult song during the first few months of life and are then isolated, the song develops normally the next spring, when the birds are about nine months old. After exposing young birds to an adult song, Konishi (1965) deafened some of the young birds. The following spring, the deafened birds failed to develop the correct patterning of vocal movements. When deafening followed song development, however, there was no immediate deficit in the song pattern.

When a bird is to learn a complex series of movements necessary to produce a song, a trace or model of how the song should sound must first be established in the bird's memory. Later, the bird makes vocal movements. These movements may not be immediately correct, and hence the song may at first be incorrect. At this stage, the bird must have auditory feedback of its own voice to compare with the internalized model in its memory. On the basis of this comparison, the bird can make changes in the movement pattern until the auditory feedback matches the model. After further practice, the auditory feedback needed for learning can be eliminated since the motor program has now been established.

Nottebohm severed the nerves that supply parts of the vocal apparatus of birds. Some segments of the movement sequence and song dropped out as a consequence of the de-innervation, but the rest was maintained. Thus, it may be concluded that neither the kinesthetic nor the auditory feedback from the missing movement segments is needed to trigger the rest of the movement pattern. The implication is that the movement sequence is centrally controlled and is not dependent on feedback.

Implications of bird song development for human skill learning. The traditional view of skill learning is that practice makes perfect. This statement, although undoubtedly true, may be misleading. The older view—that kinesthetic feedback controls the initiation of successive movements—implies that movements must be executed in order to generate feedback to trigger the next segment of the skill. The view that movements are controlled by motor programs, however, opens the possibility of a very different approach to skill learning. Perhaps, in learning some skills, the best approach is to *not* practice at all in early stages of development, or perhaps to practice only minimally. Taking a lesson from the birds, it may be more fruitful to watch, listen to, or passively move with a model for extensive periods of time until the model becomes firmly fixed in memory. Then one can begin to practice movements and compare one's own performance to the internalized model.

There is a very interesting and old approach to skill learning that is quite similar to the way in which birds learn songs. Pronko

(1969) has described the Suzuki method of teaching children in Japan to play the violin. At the time a baby is born, or shortly thereafter, the parent selects a single piece of great music, by Bach or Mozart for example, and plays a recording of it to the baby each day. It is important that the recording be of very high fidelity so that a perfect model will be stored in memory. After several months of hearing the same piece, the infant comes to recognize the music, as evidenced by the soothing effect of the music on the infant. Only then is a second piece selected. More models are gradually added to the growing child's repertoire until, at about three or four years of age, the child has several models stored in memory. He is then allowed to have a violin and is sent to school. At school, the child refines the sequences of movements he is taught until eventually he can play great music. Presumably, the child can compare the notes he produces with the precise auditory templates stored in memory and make corrections in the movement sequence that produces the sounds. Only a few years later does the child learn to read music. "Every spring," writes Pronko "in the Sports Palace in Tokyo, up to 5000 very small and very beautiful Japanese children give a fantastic mass violin concert—without rehearsal or even a fixed program. The music is such that one very old gentleman was moved to tears on hearing it. His name was Pablo Casals" (p. 52). According to Pronko, world-renowned violinists such as Toshiyo Eto and Kohi Toyoda have been trained by the Suzuki method.

Psychologists have performed some studies relevant to the discussion of internal models (see Holding 1965, chap. 3). In some studies, subjects have held a knob that was moving in a complex or well-timed pattern. Other subjects moved an implement along a groove that restricted movement. Such passive involvement in movement control sometimes yields performance on subsequent self-controlled movements that is as good as that obtained by practicing with self-controlled movements from the beginning. It remains to be seen, however, whether the internalization of models before practice is a generally useful approach to skill learning. Nevertheless, it is likely that the newer conceptions of movement control and the role of feedback will have profound effects on the manner in which skills are taught (see Posner and Keele 1972).

Summary

Fitts has shown that the time required to move a limb to a target depends both on the distance of the movement and on the target width. More precisely, Fitts's law states thatMT

$= a + (b \log_2 2D/W)$ where a and b are constants, D is distance, and W is target width. Interestingly, this formulation predicts that changes in distance and precision may cancel each other out, yielding no change in MT. This simple equation has important implications for the improvement of skilled performance. If one understands the factors that influence movements, one can select efficient motions to accomplish a task. Indeed, the approach of minimizing both distance moved and precision required is the typical method by which time-and-motion analysts attempt to improve skilled performance (see Niebel 1962). In addition to instructing people in more efficient movement, machines can also be redesigned to reduce MT.

Further inquiry has suggested that Fitts's law ultimately derives from feedback principles; the longer and more precise a movement, the more corrections are needed to hit a target. Such corrections appear to take about 200 to 250 milliseconds. Predictions of MT based on number of corrections needed to hit a target and on amount of time per correction fit very well with actual MTs found by Fitts. The feedback interpretation of movement control is also compatible with studies of the attention demands of movements. Movements requiring correction demand attention; those not requiring correction do not.

Many skills involving sequences of movement often depend on visual feedback early in practice. A movement is made, the consequences are analyzed, and a correction is made. Such skills are said to be under closed-loop control and are very jerky in appearance. With practice, the mode of control changes, and the performance becomes much smoother. Visual feedback no longer appears to control individual movements but instead appears to be used for periodic correction or continuous modulation of a preprogrammed sequence.

It is possible that control shifts from the visual to the kinesthetic system. Indeed, Fleishman and Rich have shown that kinesthetic sensitivity is increasingly important as proficiency in a motor task develops. Evidence from de-afferentation studies, however, indicates that kinesthesis may be eliminated and a skilled sequence still executed, which suggests that the sequencing and timing of at least some skills are governed by central motor programs rather than by kinesthetic feedback. Feedback is nevertheless, useful to initiate a motor program in the appropriate place, to monitor the output of a motor program for periodic corrections, and to make fine motor adjustments.

Feedback is also of use in the acquisition of motor programs. An analysis of bird song development—a skill that involves a very fine sequencing of movements—suggests that the auditory consequences of vocal movements may be compared with an internalized model of the correct sound pattern, and, on the basis of that comparison, the motor program may be readjusted until the feedback matches the standard. At that point, both the feedback and the standard can be eliminated, as long as the environment does not change. However, sensory feedback is still useful because the relationship between the organism and the environment changes occasionally. The view of motor program acquisition developed from the study of birds may have strong implications for the training of human skills.

 **Chapter 7**

ATTENTION

Earlier chapters in this book examined the attention demands involved in committing information to memory, retrieving information from memory, initiating responses, and controlling movements. Usually attention demands were assessed by determining the degree of interference between tasks, and from such observations of interference it was concluded that some mental processes require attention and others do not. A detailed examination of the conclusions about attention arising from each of these areas of study—memory storage, memory retrieval, and movement control—discloses similarities among the processes that require attention. One of the purposes of this chapter is, therefore, integrative—to point out these similarities and give a more general description of a theory of attention. Some implications of this theory for the way in which man perceives the world about him are then explored.

The study of man's processing limitations, as revealed by interference techniques, is only one important approach to attention. Because people are limited in dealing with several sources of information presented at about the same time, they select some information and reject or hold in abeyance other information. Thus, questions about *selective attention*—the way in which one message is selected and others are ignored—are also of interest. Furthermore, man's efficiency in dealing with information also depends on his degree of *alertness*—in ordinary terms, whether or not he is "paying attention." The latter half of this chapter briefly considers selectivity and alertness and some interactions between them.

A General Theory of Attention

Each of the processing tasks considered in this book can be conceptualized as involving two successive stages. The first stage consists of the reception of information through one of the sensory systems and the retrieval from memory of stored information regarding the sensory stimulation. This stage has variously been called memory retrieval, memory contact or memory activation. After retrieval of information from memory, various mental operations may be performed.[1]

Memory Retrieval and Mental Operations

At the very least, one source of activated memory may be *selected* and *perceived*. Reicher (1969) briefly exposed either a letter, a pair of unrelated letters, or a four-letter word to subjects and followed this presentation with a visual masking field to terminate short-term visual storage. A pair of test letters was then presented, and subjects were asked which of the two letters had occurred in the earlier exposure. When the first exposure involved two unrelated letters, recognition of either of the letters was worse than when the first exposure consisted of only one letter. However, when the first exposure was a four-letter word, recognition of any letter from the word was slightly better than recognition in the one-letter condition. Thus, in the Reicher paradigm, briefly presented material activated information stored in memory regarding letter names or word names. If several units are activated, then one source of activated memory can be selected and perceived for later report.

Another mental operation is *rehearsal*. When material presented for memorization is followed by an irrelevant task, memory loss occurs very rapidly. The maintenance of activated memory and transfer into long-term memory requires rehearsal, and other tasks may interfere with rehearsal. Murdock (1961) tested subjects for recall of either three unrelated letters, single words, or three unrelated words after various retention intervals during which they performed a distracting task. The single-word condition resulted in the best recall at all time intervals despite the fact that more letters occurred in the single word than in the case of the three unrelated letters. Three words were recalled as well as three unrelated letters. The Murdock study suggests that the word units

---

[1]Later in this chapter, it is suggested that mental operations may sometimes also be performed on sensory information prior to its activation.

activated in memory are rehearsed, rather than the letters comprising the units being rehearsed. One may wonder why words that are already stored in memory and are activated by their presentation need be rehearsed. The reason is that the experimental task requires the word to be stored in a new context.

Sometimes, the information retrieved from memory concerns a response, and once the information is retrieved, a response must immediately be initiated. *Response initiation* is another operation. Karlin and Kestenbaum (1968) presented subjects with two successive signals, each requiring a different response. The response to the second signal was delayed, as is the case in many other situations involving a psychological refractory period. More important, however, the delay of the second response depended primarily on the amount of time that elapsed since the first response, and not on the memory retrieval time of the second signal.

Movement correction is an operation similar to response initiation. Both can only follow a process of memory retrieval. Bruner (1968) has shown that when a discrepancy exists between the current position of a movement and the target, the necessary correction has been stored in memory. The young infant makes inappropriate movements when reaching for an object, and it is only over a period of months that proper movement corrections are learned. Corrections of a motor program, as well as movements to a target, also require that feedback be compared to internal representations of the motor program. Posner and Keele (1969) and Ells (1969) found that the task of moving a lever to a mechanical stop required no attention. On the other hand, a visually guided movement to a target did require attention. Neither movement itself nor the monitoring of feedback appears to involve attention; only the correction of movements is attention demanding.

A number of other mental operations may also occur in other situations. Information retrieved from memory may be *compared* or matched with other information that is physically present (Sternberg 1969); mental *counting* may occur (Schvaneveldt and Staudenmayer 1970); or *searches* for new information based on already retrieved information may be initiated (Brown and McNeill 1966).

Which stage takes attention? The evidence from the various studies cited above all point to the same general theory of attention. The retrieval of information stored in memory and triggered by an external stimulus does not require attention. Subsequent operations, in contrast, are attention-demanding.

To say that memory retrieval does not require attention is simply to say that if more than one source of sensory information impinges on a person at the same time, all the sources activate information stored in memory without interfering with each other. If simultaneously presented letters contacted memory sequentially, then it would take longer to perceive a letter in a word than a single letter. But Reicher found that a letter from a briefly exposed word was actually recognized better than a single-letter exposure, suggesting that all letters in the word had contacted memory simultaneously. Similarly, if individual letters comprising a word were rehearsed, then recall of the word should be as poor as recall of individual letters. But Murdock found that the several letters making up a word seem to contact memory as a unit, and it is the unit that is rehearsed for later recall. Karlin and Kestenbaum found that the delay in responding to the second of two signals was relatively unaffected by the memory retrieval time of the second signal. Therefore, the retrieval stage for the second signal appears to have overlapped with the processing of the first signal. Keele, utilizing the Stroop technique, found that memory retrieval of a neutral word did not interfere with the processing of a relevant word. Finally, a task such as walking appears to require little or no attention, even though kinesthetic feedback is, presumably, continually being matched with the memory of the motor program.

Clearly, people are limited in their ability to process information. If the limitation is not attributable to memory retrieval, then by implication it is attributable to the subsequent mental operations. Apparently, only one mental operation can be performed at a time. Two unrelated letters are not selected and perceived as well as is a four-letter word, because the unrelated letters activate two different units in memory, and it would take two selective operations to perceive them. The word is seen as a single unit, and letters in the word may be deduced from that unit. Likewise, three words are forgotten as rapidly as three unrelated letters, because in each case each of the three units requires a separate rehearsal operation. The more units there are, the less any one unit can be rehearsed, and the greater the retention loss. The delay in responding to the second of two signals depends on the amount of time that has elapsed since the first response. Apparently, some minimum time must pass after the initiation of one response and before another mental operation can occur.

Not only do mental operations of one type interfere with each other, as when the rehearsal of one unit interferes with the rehearsal of another unit, but operations of one type also interfere with operations of another type. In Murdock's study, the task of counting backward by threes interfered with the rehearsal of words or letters. Posner and Rossman (1965) found that mental operations involved in the task of classifying numbers interfered with the rehearsal of digits. Crowder (1967) reported that the operations involved in key-pressing in response to lights interfered with the rehearsal of letters. The process of correcting a movement interferes with the ability to respond to a simultaneous signal (Ells 1969). Therefore, in general, it can be said that the operations subsequent to memory retrieval require attention.

People are constantly bombarded by stimulation—too much stimulation to process completely. A processing mechanism that is limited in the stage subsequent to memory retrieval may have great advantages over a mechanism that is limited in the retrieval stage. Sensory information that has no meaning to a person is automatically gated out when selection occurs among information activated in memory since no stored unit is activated in memory. The result is a great diminution in the amount of stimulation competing for a limited selective mechanism. Furthermore, different sources of sensory stimulation may combine to elicit a single unit in memory. Letters may combine to elicit a word, for example. The result is, again, a reduction in the number of units that require access to the subsequent, limited stage of processing. People would be much less capable of interacting with their environments if the selective mechanism operated only upon sensory information rather than upon information activated in memory, because there is so much more information at the sensory level than at the more abstract memory level. S, the man described in chapter 3, who forgot essentially nothing, was so burdened by the variety of sensory experiences aroused by a stimulus that he had a very difficult time understanding conversations or material he read.

Related theories of attention. Other investigators, using somewhat different language and different sources of evidence, have also concluded that the retrieval process is essentially unlimited, and the bottleneck in processing occurs subsequent to the retrieval stage. These investigators have also made important elaborations of the theory of attention.

Consider the problem of selecting one source of information over other competing sources. If a number of units are activated simultaneously in memory, how is one singled out to be operated upon? Deutsch and Deutsch (1963) have suggested that various locations in memory are given different weightings according to their importance. The location with the highest importance gains first access to the limited stage of operations. The second most important area of activated memory is operated upon next—and so on. One evidence that selection depends on importance is Moray's (1959) observation that a person who is listening to a speech will stop listening when his name is spoken from another location. Presumably, a person's own name is very important, and the sound of his name will intrude even when he is attending to another message. The importance of a location also depends on the context in which a signal is embedded. The ring of a telephone may be very important when a call from a friend is expected. Certain words may be important, and hence likely to be selected, depending on the preceding words.

Norman (1968) and Morton (1969a) have both proposed extensions of the Deutsch and Deutsch theory. Norman has suggested that the location selected in memory is dependent on the degree of activation. The degree of activation, in turn, depends not only on the importance of the various areas in memory, but also on the strength of the input. These two factors—importance and strength of input—combine to determine which location is selected. Morton has suggested that memory activation should be viewed not as an all-or-none process, but as a gradual accumulation of information to a criterion level of activation. The memory unit that accumulates information is called a logogen. The criteria of activation in the various logogens are based on importance, just as in the Deutsch and Norman models, and the logogen that first reaches the criterion level is selected. The rate of accumulation of information in any one logogen depends both on the strength of the input and on the strength of the connection between input and logogen. The buildup of information in the logogen is also influenced by a variable background activity, upon which are superimposed the effects of a signal. (Chapter 5 gives a more detailed description of Morton's logogen model and its application to reaction time.) The logogen model is, at present, the most comprehensive model of the mechanism by which several inputs of information simultaneously activate several representations in memory, and a selection of one representation is made.

Implications for Conscious Perception

One of the great mysteries about human beings is conscious perception. Man lives in a constantly changing environment and responds in various ways to those changes. Many psychologists, such as J. B. Watson and B. F. Skinner, have been interested primarily in relating the behavior of organisms to their environmental conditions. Such an approach is called strict behaviorism. Yet most people report that they not only respond to the environment, they also consciously perceive and are aware of the world about them. Throughout history, people have been interested not only in behavior, but in the mind itself. Originally, the term *psychology* was used to denote the study of the mind. Only recently have many people come to define psychology as the study of behavior. Psychologists who are interested in information processing also study behavior, but their observations of behavior in controlled, experimental situations will, it is hoped, lead to some understanding of the mind and consciousness.

One of the most common subjective experiences of consciousness is its seriality; only one thing seems to be perceived or able to come to consciousness at a time. If this experience is accepted as universal, then the theory of attention just presented tells us something about conscious perception. If conscious perception is also limited, it may be that what people usually perceive or are consciously aware of is not sensory information but that which has been activated in memory and is currently being operated on. (Later on, some evidence will be presented that mental operations can also be performed on sensory information.)

The Whorfian hypothesis. Taken in its strongest form, the statement that man perceives that which is activated in memory means that man never has an unbiased view of the world about him. What he sees depends not only on the stimulus from the outside world but also on the information that he has stored in memory about similar stimuli. Different people perceive the same stimulus in different ways because the stimulus activates different contents in their memories.

Much the same conclusion was reached many years ago by the famous linguist, Benjamin Whorf (1940), and his view is now known as the Whorfian hypothesis. After careful study of the Hopi and Shawnee languages, Whorf concluded that the thought content of these people differed very much from that of English-speaking Americans. It was not just that the words and values of the cultures were different, but, according to Whorf, that which the people perceived was itself different:

> The world is presented in a kaleidoscopic flux of impressions which has to be organized by our minds—

> and this means largely by the linguistic systems in our
> minds. We cut nature up, organize it into concepts, and
> ascribe significance as we do, largely because we are
> parties to an agreement to organize it that way—an
> agreement that holds throughout our speech community
> and is codified in the patterns of our language. . . . We
> are thus introduced to a new principle of relativity,
> which holds that all observers are not led by the same
> physical evidence to the same picture of the universe,
> unless their linguistic backgrounds are similar, or can
> in some way be calibrated. [P. 231]

To restate Whorf's contention in another way, the world of sensation is really a continuum. But in dealing with the massive quantity of sensory events, people learn to categorize the world. Stimuli that are close together on a continuum come to evoke in memory the same categorical representation. Man's limited processing mechanism is then able to deal with categories rather than the multitude of sensory events. People in different cultures categorize the world of sensations in quite different ways, and the categories are reflected in the language of the culture. The categorizations, in turn, determine what is perceived.

Studies by Liberman and his colleagues (1967) have shown that the perception of speech sounds is indeed categorical. The consonant sounds corresponding to b, d, and g, for example, actually are on a continuum in the frequency spectrum, and apparently arbitrary boundaries differentiate b from d and d from g. For example, the b in bet and the b in bat have different frequency characteristics. Two speech sounds a certain distance apart on the frequency scale are much more difficult to discriminate when they belong to the same category (as when both are variants of b) than when they belong to two different categories (such as b and d). In other words, people appear to perceive the category that is activated by a speech sound and not the sound itself.

Two cautions should be made with regard to the Liberman findings, however. First, some categorical perception of speech sounds apparently occurs in infants only one month old (Eimas et al. 1971). If sounds are presented while an infant is sucking on a nipple, the sucking pattern usually changes when the sound is changed, indicating that the baby perceives the sound change. However, some sound alterations that, for an adult, would fall into the same speech category (such as two forms of b) do not elicit changes in sucking, suggesting that infants do not perceive certain sound alterations. For some sounds, therefore, categorical perception may not be dependent on past learning and subsequent memory activation; the categorical perception may be present from birth. Nevertheless, Brown and Lenneberg (1958) have shown differences in perception of vowel sounds by Navaho as opposed to English speakers. The implication is that at least some, but not all, of the categorical perception of speech is based on previous learning. A second caution is that a demonstration of categorical perception of speech sounds may depend on there being a small time delay between the sounds that are compared to each other. A delay forces the comparisons to be based on memory.

Darclay (1970) presented various d sounds to adults. The sounds differed in frequency, and subjects were asked to say whether a particular d sounded more like a b or more like a g. When the frequency characteristics of a d were more similar to a g than a b, subjects were more likely to say that it sounded more like a g. Thus, under some conditions, subjects are able to make some distinctions among speech sounds belonging to the same phoneme category. Perception may in some cases be based on precategorical sensory events and not just on information activated in memory. In its strongest form, the theory that a person's perceptions are completely determined by that which is stored in memory is probably incorrect. But before pursuing other evidence that conscious perception can occur prior to memory activation, let us examine a further implication of the notion of memory-limited perception.

Manipulating the contents of memory. If, under some circumstances, people perceive information activated in memory and not the sensory information that elicits the stored information, then manipulation of the stored information should change the way in which an event is perceived. There have been several attempts to demonstrate this, mostly without success. A large part of the problem appears to be that when people are responding normally to changes in the environment, they do appear to respond to information stored in memory. But when they are asked to perceive detail in individual stimuli, they are usually able to do this also. One study by Festinger, Ono, Burnham, and Bamber (1967), however, did find that manipulation of the contents of memory affected the perception of a stimulus.

One thing that may be stored in memory about a stimulus is a motor program relating the stimulus to a movement. For example, if a person sees a straight line, then stored in his memory may be a motor program that, when activated, moves his arm along the line. His arm can fairly accurately trace the line, even when his eyes are closed, after the movement has been initiated. That such a correspondence between stimulus and motor program is learned was seen in Bruner's (1968) observations of infants. Young infants have a difficult time reaching for objects; such movement control must be learned. Further, it was pointed out in chapter 6 that when the correspondence between sensory input and motor output is artificially manipulated, readjustment occurs rather rapidly (McLaughlin 1967).

In the study by Festinger and his colleagues, prisms were placed in front of the eyes of subjects. One effect of the prisms was to make straight lines appear curved. If a person were to try to move his finger rapidly along a straight line immediately after having prisms placed before his eyes, he would have difficulty doing so. Eventually, however, a new motor program would be developed in response to the stimulus. In other words, the contents of memory would be changed to a small degree. Instead of eliciting in memory an old but now inappropriate "curved" motor program, the curved stimulus would now elicit a "straight" program for controlling the limb.

To test the question of whether such a change in motor program changes the way the stimulus looks, a pair of vertically aligned brass rods one-half inch apart were placed before the subjects. By turning a knob with his hand, a subject could set the rods either apparently straight or at varying degrees of apparent curvature, as viewed through a prism. The degree of apparent curvature was assessed by setting the rods in a straight position and asking the subjects to twist the knob until the lines looked straight. After the apparent curvature was assessed, the rods were reset in a straight position so that they again looked curved to the subjects. The subjects were then asked to move a stylus between the rods. In one case, the subjects were to move the stylus rapidly and try to avoid touching the rod on either side of the stylus. This would, of course, require that a new motor program be adopted. In another case, the subjects were to press the stylus firmly against one rod and move it down. This would not require the adoption of a new motor program, since the pressure of contact would guide the movement.

After a series of trials, the subjects were again tested for amount of apparent curvature of the rods as viewed through prisms. In both cases, the straight rods appeared less curved than they had before the movement trials. But, most important, the greatest change in apparent curvature occurred for the subjects who had had to develop a new motor program in response to the stimulus. In other words, alteration of the contents of memory—in this case a motor program—altered perception of a sensory event.

Other studies attempting to manipulate experimentally the contents of memory have not succeeded in showing a change in conscious perception, apparently because the mechanism of conscious perception is very flexible. Perception can apparently be focused at the level of sensory information and mental operations performed at that level, or it can be focused after memory activation. A technique developed by Posner and colleagues has presented good evidence for the multiple-level flexibility of perception.

The Posner studies of levels of consciousness. People often make judgments about the things they perceive. They may, for example, decide whether or not two objects they see are identical. One way of doing this might be to compare the representations activated in memory of the two objects. On the other hand, if the objects not only have the same representation in memory but are also nearly identical in shape, the judgment might occur prior to memory activation and be based on the sensory properties of the objects.

To determine whether perceptual judgments can be based on sensory information prior to categorization, Posner and Mitchell (1967) selected as visual objects pairs of letters. For each pair of letters, subjects were to judge whether or not the letters were the same, and their reaction time was measured. Although other visual objects could have been chosen, letters are ideal for the purpose because certain letter forms are very different in shape but have the same categorical representation. For example, *A* and *a* are physically very different but have the same name. The shapes *A* and *A* not only have the same name, but they are also physically identical. In contrast, two shapes such as *A* and *B* are different both physically and in name.

If people can make perceptual judgments on the basis of sensory information, then it might be expected that shapes that are physically identical could be judged as being the same faster than shapes that are physically different but have the same name. Posner and Mitchell found that physically identical letters are typically judged to be the same about seventy to ninety milliseconds faster than letters that have different shapes but the same name. In another of Posner and Mitchell's experiments, it was found that nonsense forms previously unfamiliar to the subjects were judged as being physically identical as fast as were letters with which the usbjects had had years of experience in everyday life.

Conclusions about consciousness. It has been assumed that consciousness is limited in the sense that only one thing can be perceived at a time. Because people can perform only one mental operation at a time subsequent to memory retrieval, it has been suggested that the content of consciousness is that which is activated in memory *and* operated upon. This notion is somewhat similar to the Whorfian hypothesis that people's perceptions are constrained by their language and culture. Supporting this idea is evidence that the perception of speech sounds, at least, is dependent on learned categories. Furthermore, there is some evidence, albeit rather weak, that experimental manipulation of the contents of memory results in perceptual changes. It is absurd, however, to suppose that only events that activate information in memory are perceivable. Certainly, nonsense forms never before experienced can be perceived. Posner and Mitchell showed, in addition, that mental operations can be performed on sensory information faster than they can be performed upon information stored in memory.

The conclusion emerges, then, that when several signals impinge upon the human organism, they simultaneously activate their representations in memory. Mental operations can be performed on the information either at the sensory level, prior to memory activation, or at the level of memory. In either case, mental operations (except memory retrieval itself) interfere with each other—that is, they demand attention. In a weak form, the Whorfian hypothesis appears to be correct. People do perceive the world in terms of their stored memories if mental operations are being performed at that level. However, they can also perform, and presumably be conscious of, mental operations performed on sensory information. Moreover, there is no evidence indicating that selection of one signal at a sensory level blocks a second signal from simultaneous access to memory.

What useful functions would be served by a flexible mechanism that allows conscious perception to occur at different levels? There are no clear answers to this question yet. It has been suggested that selection at the level of memory can lead to conflict and mistakes. In the case of the Stroop effect, for example, a color of ink as a stimulus activates a color name at the level of memory; a color word does the same. In order to decide which of two competing color names one should respond to, one must determine from sensory information which is the color stimulus and which is the color word. In some situations, mental operations performed on sensory information yield faster responses than operations performed on information stored in memory, as shown in the Posner and Mitchell study.

In an earlier chapter, it was suggested that people can generate a visual image from an auditory input. Such an image can then

be compared with objects perceived visually when one is searching rapidly for some particular object. Thus, the flexibility of
the level of conscious perception allows vastly improved efficiency in information processing. When perception occurs at the
more abstract level of memory, less information requires access
to the limited stage of operations, and processing is speeded up.
However, when processing at an abstract level results in ambigui-
ty and error, selection can be shifted to the sensory level.

Selective Attention

When several locations in memory are simultaneously activated, a problem arises in determining which of the
competing activated memories should be selected. According to
the logogen model, the area of activated memory first reaching
some criterion level is selected, and the criterion level may be
predetermined. There may be a relatively permanent and low
criterion level for one's own name and a few other items. The
logogen corresponding to an expected event may have a temporarily low criterion. But how is selection made in the common
circumstance when there are no prior reasons determining the
relative importance of events? If two or more people in the same
room are talking at the same time, and a listener is trying to
understand one person and ignore the others, how does the selective mechanism operate? To say that the words of the desired
speaker are more important than the words of other speakers
does not help unless there is some way of knowing in advance
what words the desired speaker is apt to say.

One possible mechanism of making rapid adjustments in criteria and hence in selective attention is to utilize the context
of the message. If a desired speaker is talking about sports, then
the logogens connected with sports may have a lowered criterion.
In addition, within a single sentence, the use of a word or group
of words makes other words or meanings likely to occur next.
In other words, language is redundant, and redundancy may be
used to change criteria continually.

To determine whether context and the statistical properties of
language are sufficient for selection, Cherry (1953) had the same
person record two different prose passages. The two messages
were then played back simultaneously through a single loudspeaker, so that the redundancy of the messages was all that
distinguished one message from the other. Under these conditions, the listener was able to repeat back one of the messages,
but only with extreme difficulty. A playback often had to be

repeated ten or more times before the subject could separate the two messages. Apparently, the criteria of various logogens can be rapidly adjusted with changing context to improve selection of the intended message, but really efficient selection is not possible purely on the basis of context and redundancy.

The Cocktail Party Phenomenon

When several persons are speaking at a time, it is obviously easier to select one speaker than can be explained by the context and redundancy of language. The ability to attend selectively to one person's speech in the presence of competing messages is called the cocktail party phenomenon. Two factors that may explain the phenomenon are the physical locations of the voices and the different frequency characteristics of different voices.

In the earliest test of this hypothesis, Cherry (1953) simultaneously played two prose passages through separate earphones, so that one message went to each ear of the subjects. The subjects were quite easily able to repeat one message and ignore the other. Of course, in natural settings, messages usually come from different physical locations rather than through different ears. To simulate this condition, Spieth, Curtis, and Webster (1954) simultaneously played two messages spoken by the same person but delivered through separate loudspeakers. When the speakers were in an adjoining position, the subjects had very little ability to understand the messages. When the loudspeakers were separated, however, the ability of subjects to select the designated message increased dramatically.

In another part of their study, Spieth and his colleagues put frequency filters over the loudspeakers. One of the verbal messages was presented with the voice frequencies below 1600 cycles per second filtered out. The other loudspeaker passed only voice frequencies below 1600 cycles per second. With this great frequency difference, separation of the two messages was quite efficient, even when the loudspeakers were next to each other.

Thus, apparently, people at a cocktail party are able to attend selectively to one particular speaker because the context of his speech increases the importance of some words and makes it easier for him to be identified. Further, and more important, speakers are usually located in different parts of the room, and the frequency characteristics of their voices differ. Without these cues, people would be hopelessly lost in trying to listen to one person while others are talking at the same time.

The Filter Theory of Broadbent and Treisman

One possible mechanism accounting for a person's ability to attend selectively to one auditory message while ignoring others is a filter that blocks messages having certain physical features (such as location or frequency) and keeps them from contacting memory. Such a model was postulated by Broadbent (1957, 1958). In Broadbent's terms, a filter can select one "channel" of information and filter another. One way to conceive of such a filter is in terms of neural inhibition; neurons that carry certain frequencies, for example, might be inhibited. An implication of Broadbent's filter model is that people should be unable to remember the content of an ignored auditory message, since the message would be filtered out prior to having elicited any meaning. The only exceptions would be cases in which the message being attended to did not require all the available processing time, and some switching from one channel of input to another occurred. Indeed, Cherry (1953) found that when one message was directed to one ear and the other message to the other ear, subjects did not notice some rather drastic changes in the ignored message. They did not notice when the signal switched from English to German or when the tape on which the ignored message was recorded was reversed and played backward. They did notice, however, when the ignored message switched from a male voice to either a tone or a female voice. This last finding is consistent with filter theory, since the filter is based on the frequency characteristics of the ignored message. If the frequency were shifted, the filter would have to be readjusted.

Although some of the evidence is consistent with a filter theory, other evidence contradicts it. A study by Moray (1959), for example, showed that people often noticed their spoken name while they were listening to another message, and this is true even if their name is spoken from another location or in a different frequency from the message to which they are attending. In Treisman's (1964) study with French-English bilinguals, a message in English which subjects were to repeat was played into one ear, and a message in French which subjects were to ignore was played into the other ear. At first, the French and English messages were different, but after a period of time, the French message was switched to a French translation of the English message. When the ignored French version just slightly lagged behind the English version, the majority of subjects noticed that both messages had the same meaning.

Treisman suggested that the ignored message, rather than being completely blocked, is attenuated. If a message is important (such as one's name) or becomes likely in the context of an ongoing message being attended to, it can be detected even though it is weakened. Thus, French words in the ignored message could be perceived, even though attenuated, when they fit into the context of the English message. This more sophisticated version of filter theory is called the Broadbent-Treisman filter model of selective attention.

A critique of filter theory. The Broadbent-Treisman model seems to contradict the model of attention proposed in the first part of this chapter—that sensory information from all sources activates representations in memory without interference, and that the limited selection process occurs subsequent to memory retrieval. The Broadbent-Treisman model, on the other hand, claims that sensory information from ignored sources is either filtered out or attenuated prior to memory contact; the limitation occurs at the memory retrieval stage.

In an important although not definitive study performed by Lewis (1970), subjects were presented with simultaneous pairs of words, one to each ear, and asked to repeat as fast as possible the words played into one ear and ignore the words played into the other ear. Subjects were never able to recall the ignored words. However, unknown to the listener, the ignored word in a pair was occasionally a synonym of the word being attended to. When such a synonym occurred in the ignored message, the RT for repetition of the word attended to increased. When the ignored word was an antonym, the RT decreased. Lewis's study, therefore, presents strong evidence that the ignored word was not filtered out prior to memory retrieval, since its meaning affected the time required to repeat the item being attended to.

It should be pointed out that context effects cannot account for the Lewis results as they can for Treisman's results. In Lewis's study, successive pairs of words were unrelated, so one word could not be used to predict subsequent words. It should also be noted that the simple fact that a word contacts memory does not mean that it will be stored for later recall. As emphasized earlier, storage appears to require a mental operation of rehearsal, which requires attention. In Lewis's study, the ignored words contacted memory, but apparently they were not rehearsed because of interference from the repetition task, and hence they could not be recalled later. Although Lewis's results are inconsistent with a pure filter theory, it is possible that an attenuation theory could fit the data. Even though the ignored message is attenuated, it could exert some influence on the activation of information stored in memory, thereby affecting RT.

An unresolved dilemma.   The discussion so far leaves us with a gap in our knowledge of selective attention. It is clear that when competing auditory messages occur, differences in location of the sound source and differences in frequency characteristics of the sound help the listener select one message and ignore the others. However, if selectivity occurs at the level of physical characteristics of the message, why does the meaning of the ignored message affect response to the selected message? If, on the other hand, selectivity occurs at the level of activated memory, why do physical characteristics of the sound, namely direction and frequency, affect selection?

Treisman (1971) recently noted the same paradox. She found that when a list of words was presented alternately, first a word to one ear and then a word to the other ear, recall was worse than when all the words were presented to both ears. This is just what would be expected if the messages received by one ear were filtered out, while those received by the other ear were selected, so that with alternate presentations attention would have to be switched back and forth between the ears. On the other hand, Treisman points out that the messages received by one ear cannot have been filtered out, since, under certain circumstances, messages from the two ears merged. For example, if the nonsense syllable *taz* were presented to one ear and *gik* to the other, the messages might merge, and the subject might perceive *tak*.

This dilemma has not been satisfactorily resolved. Certainly, much evidence indicates that multiple sources of information contact memory simultaneously. On the other hand, much evidence also indicates that selectivity is improved when an auditory message comes from a particular direction or has a particular frequency. The theory that an ignored message may be attenuated rather than filtered out may be a partial explanation, but it is not clear that the attenuation theory accounts for all the data.

Alertness

Another dimension of attention, in addition to processing capacity and selectivity, is alertness. At one extreme, a person may be in a deep sleep, and his ability to process information will be severely limited. In chapter 3 it was reported that people seem to be unable to store verbal material in memory while they are in a deep sleep. At the other extreme of alertness, a person may have just been warned that a signal to be processed is imminent, and he is highly *prepared*.

Preparation

People may be more efficient in processing information if they have prior warning of imminent events. The runner, for example, starts faster when the starting gun is preceded by a warning. Do warning signals always help performance? At a superficial level, the answer is simply yes. A warning signal just prior to a very brief or weak exposure of a stimulus enhances the detection of the signal. Similarly, when a stimulus is easily detected but speed of reaction is critical, a warning signal usually reduces the RT.

Bertelson (1967) and Bertelson and Tisseyre (1968) attempted to determine the optimum amount of time by which a warning should precede a signal to be processed. They presented a click at varying times ranging from 0 to 300 milliseconds before the onset of one of two lights. In a control case, no warning signal preceded the light. Since about five seconds elapsed between successive trials, five seconds can be viewed as the warning interval in the control condition. When about 200 milliseconds intervened between the warning signal and the reaction signal, RT was reduced by about 40 milliseconds to 60 milliseconds. Even when the warning signal occurred simultaneously with the stimulus signal, however, some reduction in RT occurred. A warning was also effective whether the warning interval was regular and predictable or whether it varied from trial to trial. It would appear, therefore, that in some instances a few hundred milliseconds of warning preceding a signal causes an improvement in decision time. A greater or lesser amount of warning time is less effective. In other instances, however, the optimum warning interval may be as much as half a second, but warning still improves RT.

A further question may be raised as to whether the increase in efficiency caused by a warning signal incurs a cost, in a manner analogous to the speed-accuracy trade-off investigated by Hick (1952). (See chapter 5 for a discussion of this issue.) An analysis of Bertelson's data indicates that as RT improved, errors increased. In a more detailed analysis of this problem, Posner, Buggie and Summers (1971) confirmed that an alerting signal, while decreasing RT, reliably increased errors. Again we see that very basic limitations of information processing are extremely difficult to overcome. Hick showed that highly motivated people can increase their reaction time, but errors also increase, and there is no overall change in the rate of information transmission. Now we see that preparation induced by a warning signal may decrease the time required to make rapid decisions, but this improvement is accompanied by an increase in errors.

Of course, in practical situations, warning signals may be more useful. Even when an increase in errors occurs, the number of errors may still be low. In many situations, speed is of greater importance than accuracy, and when errors do occasionally occur, they can often be corrected at no cost. Furthermore, in everyday situations less controlled than the laboratory setting, warning signals may actually improve information processing. A warning may cause a person to look around so that he is more likely to perceive visually presented signals. When a signal is likely to occur in a particular place, the warning may cause a person to fixate on that area. Finally, warning signals may encourage a person to interrupt temporarily another task that might interfere with the processing of a more critical signal.

Maintenance of Alertness

Many tasks in modern society—perhaps too many—are repetitive and have little variation to break the monotony. Other tasks involve long periods of vigilance, and only an occasional event occurs that requires some action. An inspector may watch an assembly line continuously for infrequent flaws; a fire lookout may scan the forest for days or months, only rarely detecting a fire; a radar watcher may watch a screen for an hour or so at a time and only occasionally see a plane that needs to be reported. People who perform such tasks must be constantly alert to avoid missing important events or suffering lapses in performance.

A typical laboratory task requiring vigilance is the jump clock test. A clock hand may skip around the clock face at one jump per second. Very infrequently, perhaps twenty-four times per hour, the hand jumps two spaces, and the subject's task is to detect the double jumps. Since the times at which the double jumps will occur are unpredictable, continuous monitoring is necessary. Another continuous task often studied is a five-choice, serial RT task. This task involves five lights and five response buttons. When a light is turned on, the subject is to tap the corresponding button to extinguish the light; another light comes on immediately; and so on. The subject steadily taps the buttons, thus extinguishing the lights, for perhaps half an hour without rest.

Many studies of vigilance and continuous key-pressing tasks have found a substantial decrement in performance over a half-hour or hour period, with most of the decrement occurring in the first ten minutes or so. On the vigilance task, fewer and fewer detections of the infrequent signals are made as time passes. For continuous, repetitive tasks, the rate of response declines as time passes; there is an increase in the number of short periods during which the subject does not respond at all; and the number of response errors increases.

Sleep loss, noise, and alcohol. Wilkinson and colleagues have carried out an extensive series of studies of performance decrement with various stressors. In one study (Wilkinson 1963), subjects performed the five-choice, serial RT task described above. The task was performed either in the presence of an intense noise (one hundred decibels) or in relative quiet. Further, the subjects performed either with normal amounts of sleep or with thirty-two hours of sleep deprivation. Figure 26 shows the proportion of response errors in successive, ten-minute blocks of time for the various groups. (The results tabulating number of correct responses and periods of time in which no responses occurred were similar.) When subjects had had a normal amount of sleep, a high level of noise caused increasing deterioration in performance over successive ten-minute periods. Similarly, when subjects performed in a quiet environment but were sleep-deprived, there was an accelerated decrement in performance over time. But, surprisingly, subjects who performed during intense noise and who were sleep-deprived had fewer errors than subjects who performed under conditions of sleep deprivation only!

Quite clearly, noise and sleep deprivation affect performance of repetitive tasks in different ways, such that they tend to cancel each other out. Wilkinson suggests that noise tends to arouse people physiologically. Since, under normal sleep conditions, people are already at an optimal level of arousal, intense noise results in overarousal and, consequently, a decrement in performance. Sleep deprivation, on the other hand, results in underarousal, which also causes performance decrement. The presence of noise arouses a sleepy person toward the optimum level.

More recently, Wilkinson and Colquhoun (1968) looked at the joint effects of alcohol and sleep deprivation on serial RT. With

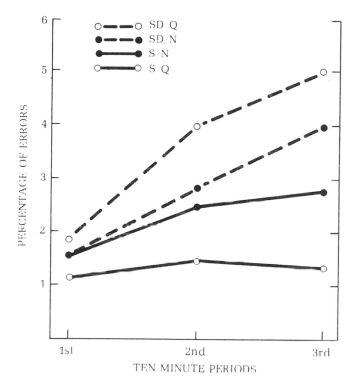

Figure 20. Percentage of responses in error in an RT task performed in quiet (Q) and noise (N) and with normal sleep (S) or sleep deprivation (SD). (From Wilkinson. 1963)

normal amounts of sleep, the consumption of alcohol, as might be expected, caused a decrement in performance. When subjects were deprived of sleep for thirty-two hours, however, a more complex pattern of results emerged. Even though all subjects had consumed the same dosage of alcohol, they differed in the level of blood alcohol, as estimated by a Breathalyzer. Subjects who had low levels of blood alcohol and were sleep-deprived actually performed better than subjects who were sleep-deprived but had consumed no alcohol. In sharp contrast, subjects who had high levels of blood alcohol performed much worse than sleep-deprived subjects who had consumed no alcohol. Thus, it appears that alcohol has the dual role of arouser and depressant at different concentrations in the bloodstream. More research along the line of Wilkinson's is needed, however, to define better the effects of alcohol.

The loss of alertness caused by sleep deprivation is partially countered by the presence of noise and in some cases by the consumption of alcohol. But much more effective in countering declines in alertness are the introduction of variety to the task and periodic appraisals of performancce. When subjects are informed of their speed and errors, there is very little decline in performance over a period of half an hour on the serial RT task (Wilkinson 1963). If a person is sleepy and performance is to be maintained, then he should have a task that changes once in awhile, he should have occasional breaks, and he should constantly be informed of how well he is doing.

Pollution and sustained performance. During the last few years people have become increasingly aware of environmental problems, including pollution. Most people have been concerned with the effects of pollution on health, on aesthetics, and on the ecosystem. Few have attempted to study the effects of pollutants on man's ability to cope with his environment—that is, his ability to process information. The most widely studied pollutant has been noise, but even on this topic there have been neglected questions. Usually only very intense noise—ninety decibels or more—has been shown to affect alertness and performance adversely. But what about lower levels of noise to which people are subjected at all hours of the day? Does prolonged, low-level noise have detrimental effects on alertness and efficiency?

Studies of pollution levels that are not so extreme as to cause easily noticeable health problems could be very important, since people are subjected to low levels of pollution much of the time. In one study, Lewis, Baddeley, Bonham, and Lovett (1970) examined performances on a vigilance task, on rapid addition, on sentence comprehension, and on digit-copying of subjects who inhaled two types of air—"pure" air or air pumped in from a nearby, moderately busy road. Performance on all tasks except digit-copying showed a 15 to 20 percent impairment when the polluted air was inhaled. The implication is that air pollution caused by automobiles may be a factor in traffic accidents, since breathing polluted air impairs mental efficiency. Efficiency in the performance of other mental tasks may also be impaired by the inhalation of polluted air.

Interaction of Alertness with Selectivity and Processing Capacity

Although processing capacity, selective attention, and alertness are different dimensions of attention, they may not be independent of one another. Research on interactions between the various dimensions of attention is quite new, and some insights are just becoming available.

It has been noted that noise compensates to some degree for sleep loss, theoretically by increasing alertness. Noise also affects selectivity. Hockey (1970a, 1970b) had subjects perform a continuous tracking task, in which they followed a moving dot with a second dot by moving a handle. Simultaneous with the tracking task was a vigilance task in which subjects were to watch for brief flashes of light in front of them and to the sides. Such tasks are much like many everyday tasks. For example, the tracking task is very similar to driving, and the vigilance task is similar to the way in which people watch for important events in the periphery of their visual field while driving. Intense noise actually helped subjects maintain performance on the tracking task over a forty-minute period, but at the same time, it resulted in a decrement in the ability to detect rarely occurring light flashes. Hockey suggested that the noise resulted not only in increased arousal but also in an increased focusing of attention on the primary task to the detriment of the other. If noise increases arousal and arousal improves focusing attention, then it is possible that the presence of noise can actually help one ignore other distracting material rather than causing performance to be even worse in an already distracting situation.

Houston (1969) used the Stroop effect (discussed in chap. 5) to test the focusing hypothesis. The subjects were to name a list of colors as fast as possible. When the stimulus colors printed out conflicting color words, there was great interference in the color-naming task. When a variety of noises with an average intensity of seventy decibels were added, performance improved. In a control case, when there were no conflicting color words, distracting noise resulted in poorer performance.

Noise, therefore, appears to have a dual effect. For some tasks, noise degrades performance, probably because it results in a greater than optimal level of arousal. Noise is beneficial, however, when a person is sleepy. At the same time, either the attempt to gate out noise or the increased arousal caused by noise leads to increased focusing of attention. The result is that secondary tasks to which little attention is directed show a performance decrement. However, the increased selectivity may improve performance on the main task. The study of interactions among processing capacity, selectivity, and alertness promises to be a fruitful area of research.

 Chapter 8

A VIEW OF MAN

While direct technological consequences often flow from basic research in the physical sciences, the implications of research in the social sciences are often very different. Research and theory in the social sciences may influence our view of the nature of man, and our view of man, in turn, may have broad social implications. Freudian theory, for instance, is not just a theory of personality and memory; it suggests that man's actions are often determined by unconscious processes rather than by deliberate intent. Freud's views have greatly changed our notions of social responsibility and may have influenced our concept of judicial and penal institutions to change from punishment-oriented to rehabilitation-oriented systems.

The study of information processing—overlapping as it does with both the physical and the social sciences—has both technological and social implications. Applications to technology are quite straightforward; the design of many machines and consumer products could be improved by a consideration of human processing limitations. More general applications to social problems have only recently been attempted. Alvin Toffler, in *Future Shock*, vigorously expounds the view that increasingly rapid changes in social structures and consumer products are causing people to be faced with too many choices and are overloading their processing capacity. As a result, many people are unable to adapt, and are continuously under stress. Caution should be observed, however, in considering social applications of information processing theory. Analogies between processing limitations discovered in the laboratory and problems in the real world are usually loose, and careful research linking the concepts from the two areas is in short supply. Nevertheless, the potential for important social applications exists, and it is useful to point out some directions these applications might take.

Technological Applications

In earlier societies, man interacted with the environment rather directly. In many modern settings, however, machines mediate between man and the environment. A person's efficiency in responding to his setting depends not just on the efficiency of the machinery at his disposal, but on how well it is matched to his processing limitations. This much neglected factor in machine design greatly curtails the potential usefulness of many man-machine systems. During World War II, for example, airplanes were often not designed with compatible and standardized control-display relationships, and numerous accidents resulted.

The importance of proper machine design extends beyond industrial and commercial uses to the everyday consumer. There is scarcely a machine or tool available to the consumer that does not suffer from being imperfectly matched to human processing capabilities. Thus, consumer interest can be forwarded not merely by exposing fraud, but by insuring that products are properly designed. There is a vast literature on design principles (see, for example, Morgan, Cook, Chapanis, and Lund 1963). Two examples will illustrate the way in which failures to consider processing limitations have resulted in bad design. Both are common consumer products—the telephone and the typewriter.

Typewriter Design

The modern typewriter was developed in 1873 and first marketed by Remington in 1874. Many facets of the design have remained unchanged since that time. The arrangement of the letters on the keyboard is basically the same. The type of key stroke is the same, although the force and distance of the strokes have been reduced on electric typewriters.

The beginning typist must store in long-term memory the correspondence between letter and key. Once such storage is accomplished, he can begin typing. When a letter or word is presented, information concerning the appropriate key to strike must be retrieved, and an appropriate movement must be executed. Reduction in the time required for any of these tasks—storage, retrieval, or movement—increases typing speed.

From this viewpoint, it can immediately be seen that the format of the standard typewriter is not carefully matched to human processing capacities. The arrangement of the letters is quite arbitrary. If the letters were arranged alphabetically, for example, the keyboard certainly would be much easier to commit to long-term memory, and this would reduce the storage time. Whether such an arrangement would reduce retrieval time and movement time for the more experienced typist is a matter to be determined. Alternately, the keyboard might be arranged in a way that would take advantage of the statistical structure of language; letters that tend to follow each other in natural language could be next to each other on the keyboard. This would probably also facilitate the initial storage process, and it might facilitate retrieval and movement. Or the keys could be arranged in a way that would minimize movement distance. With the standard format, some of the most frequent letters (such as E, T, and B) require long movements, while less frequent symbols (such as J, K, and ;) require only short movements.

Fogel (1963, pp. 406-7), in discussing typewriter designs, reported that the composer, Dvořák, designed a keyboard for one-handed amputees. By taking advantage of the statistical properties of language, he devised a keyboard on which one-handed persons could type faster than the average two-handed typist could type using the standard keyboard.

A much more radical keyboard design was studied by Conrad and Longman (1965). A primary problem with the standard keyboard is that the fingers must be lifted from some keys and moved to others in order to type. From Fitts's law, it is known that such movements take time. Conrad and Longman, therefore, proposed a basic ten-key arrangement allowing twenty-five different letters to be typed without moving the fingers or thumbs from the keys. Each letter required that two keys be pressed simultaneously, one key with the left hand and one key with the right hand. Numbers could also be accommodated in this design by using a shift key to change the function of the keys. A further innovation of Conrad and Longman was to assign letters to the keys in an orderly arrangement. If the five keys on the left hand were designated 1, 2, 3, 4, and 5 from left to right, and the keys on the right hand were designated A, B, C, D, and E, then the letter a required that keys 1 and A be pressed simultaneously; b required 1B; c required 1C; and so on. For f, the keys 2A were used; for g, 2B; and so on.

Conrad and Longman trained novice typists on their new chord design and another group on the standard design. Each group was given thirty-three sessions of training. By the tenth session, the group on the chord design had satisfactorily learned the keyboard. About twenty sessions were required to learn the standard format. By the thirty-third session, the chord group was typing faster by only about five letters per minute. The chord design therefore yielded a saving in training time but little difference in final speed.

Levy (reported in Conrad and Longman) suggested another type of chord design. Five fingers can yield thirty-one *combinations* of key presses—five one-finger responses, ten two-finger combinations, ten three-finger combinations, five four-finger combinations, and a response using all five fingers at once. Thus, it is possible for a single hand resting on only five keys to type thirty-one symbols, depending on which fingers are activated simultaneously. In the Levy design, letters are typed in pairs. The left hand, resting on one five-key keyboard, types the first letter of the pair, and the right hand, resting on the other keyboard, types the second letter. Fingers on both hands are pressed simultaneously. Although no formal experimentation was conducted, preliminary results on the Levy design indicate that high typing speeds can be attained.

Telephone Design

Speed is typically of secondary importance in dialing a telephone. More critical is the ability to dial without error. The time required to dial a typical seven-digit telephone number is very close to the immediate memory span, so by the time the first few digits are dialed, the last ones may be forgotten. One way of improving the system was suggested by Shepard and Sheenan (1965). Most telephone numbers consist of a prefix of three digits familiar to the local community and a suffix of four digits peculiar to the exchange being dialed. Despite the fact that the prefix is familiar and not likely to be forgotten, it is always dialed before the less familiar suffix, resulting in forgetting of the latter. Shepard and Sheenan found that fewer errors were made and less time was required when the familiar digits were dialed last rather than first. They suggested that the order in which numbers are listed in telephone directories is correct. If the unfamiliar digits are the last read but the first dialed, fewer errors should result. (See Posner's 1964*b* study on order of recall from short-term memory.)

A second approach to reducing dialing errors is to reduce the time that it takes to dial. The longer that material remains in short-term memory, the greater is the chance of error. Phones are now available with pushbuttons instead of the standard circular dial, and this newer format is faster and results in fewer errors. However, questions can be raised as to what layout is most compatible with previous habits of utilizing numbers. Two pushbutton formats are the adding machine layout and the telephone layout:

Adding Machine	Telephone
7 8 9	1 2 3
4 5 6	4 5 6
1 2 3	7 8 9
0	0

Conrad and Hull (1968) compared the two layouts on both speed and accuracy of keying eight-digit sequences and found the telephone layout to result in significantly fewer errors.

Conclusion

It is probably unreasonable to expect that typewriter keyboards will be radically redesigned, even if a more efficient design is discovered. There is too much investment of training and equipment in current designs. It is also unlikely that telephone networks will be altered so that the prefix digits can be dialed after the less familiar suffix digits. The pushbutton format is available, however. Of course, it is not impossible to implement extremely expensive and time-consuming changes in order to facilitate efficient information processing. The British conversion to the metric system is one example, and the adoption of unit pricing on many consumer products is another. Both the metric system and unit pricing are useful solely because they decrease the demand on processing capacities.

It is the first stages of product design, however, that should give deep consideration to human processing limitations. Many mismatched man-machine systems could be remedied. Examine the family automobile. Are knob and dial layouts standardized from one manufacturer to another to avoid confusion? Are knobs for different functions easily distinguishable, and are they able to be reached easily? Is the clutch-gearshift-brake-accelerator-steering system as efficient as a simple joy stick that can be moved front, back, left, or right to determine direction and acceleration? Examine the kitchen stove. Is the arrangement of knobs and burners compatible, so that the correct knob is easy to determine? Examine the single-edge razor. Does it require more motion than a double-edge razor, thus increasing shaving time? These products and innumerable others make greater demands on human information processing than is necessary. The result is a loss in speed, an increase in errors, often a sacrifice in safety, and unneeded annoyance.

Population and Urbanization

The world's population is increasing at a very rapid rate. At current growth rates, world population will double in about thirty-five years. Growing even faster than population is the concentration of people in cities. Among the many problems associated with these related trends are fears that the quality of life is being degraded. But quality of life is a very nebulous concept. In the words of a well-known social psychologist, Stanley Milgram (1970, p. 1462), "psychology needs an idea that links the individual's experience to the demographic circumstances of urban life."

Milgram's Analysis of the City

One of the outstanding characteristics of a large city is the number of people with whom an individual comes into contact. Milgram cites data from the Regional Plan Association that in Nassau County, a suburb of New York City, one can encounter 11,000 people in a ten-minute walking radius. In Newark, New Jersey, one can encounter 20,000 people in that time. The number increases tenfold in Manhattan; 220,000 people are accessible within a ten-minute walk. This vast number of accessible people in a large central city means a vast amount of information impinging on a person. Since people have a limited processing ability, much of this information overload cannot be dealt with effectively, and adaptations are necessary. To quote from Milgram:

> One link is provided by the concept of overload. This term, drawn from systems analysis, refers to a system's inability to process inputs from the environment because there are too many inputs for the system to cope with, or because successive inputs come so fast that input A cannot be processed when input B is pre-

> sented. When overload is present adaptations occur.
> The system must set priorities and make choices. *A*
> may be processed first while *B* is kept in abeyance, or
> one input may be sacrificed altogether. City life, as we
> experience it, constitutes a continuous set of encounters
> with overload, and of resulting adaptations. [P. 1462]

Existence in any environment requires adaptations suitable to the information load in that environment, and a large city is no exception; mechanisms that limit the information load are necessary. If a person dealt with every crisis he encountered on the way to work in Manhattan, he would seldom make it to work. Milgram suggests that one mechanism for coping with overload is to allocate less time to each input, so that each is dealt with more superficially. There is no time to exchange pleasantries with each stranger; businesslike transactions, therefore, may be more expedient. A second mechanism for coping with overload is to establish priorities—to block out less important inputs. One can employ receptionists, avoid looking at people, and so on. A third mechanism is to reverse demands so that the processing burden falls on someone else. For example, the commuter may be required to have exact change, thus freeing the bus driver from a processing demand. Another mechanism is to set up formal institutions to deal with much of the input. As Milgram notes (p. 1462), "welfare departments handle the financial needs of a million individuals in New York City, who would otherwise create an army of mendicants continuously importuning the pedestrian."

Milgram reported several studies to determine whether New Yorkers have adopted mechanisms to reduce overload. In the first study, conducted by Altman, Levine, Nadien and Villena, either a male or a female experimenter came to the door of a strange household, explained that he had lost the address of a friend who lived nearby, and asked to come in and use the phone. The requests were made at households either in Manhattan or in small towns surrounding the city. Table 6 shows the percentage of experimenters that were allowed to enter the dwellings. Females were allowed more entries than males, but, more important for our purposes, fewer entries were allowed in the city than in the small towns. This is exactly what would be expected if city dwellers had adopted mechanisms for blocking out low priority input. However, it may also be that it is more dangerous to allow strangers into one's house in the city.

In a second study, conducted by McKenna and Morgenthau,

Table 6   Percentage of Entries into City and Small-town Dwellings

Experimenter	City	Town
Male	14	50
Female	40	93

experimenters telephoned people either at home or at work in the cities of Chicago, New York, and Philadelphia, and in small towns. The caller said that he had been connected with a wrong number and then asked for information about the weather. He then asked the respondent to hold the line for a minute. If the respondent remained on the line, the caller asked for the telephone number of a hotel or motel. Even though there was no danger to the respondents, people living in the city were less helpful than people living in towns.

The studies Milgram reports provide some support for the proposal that inhabitants of large cities adopt methods to shelter themselves from information overload. Such mechanisms may continue to operate regardless of whether information capacity is overloaded at the moment. People may be rude not deliberately but because rudeness is a habitual way to cope with information overload. However, Milgram's studies involved residents of New York, and New Yorkers may tend to be more uncooperative than residents of other large cities. Furthermore, any tendency to be uncooperative may derive from causes other than information overload. Nonetheless, Milgram's results suggest that the information processing concept may be useful in understanding the ways in which people adapt to urban environments, and this understanding may be helpful in defining optimum city sizes.

Cravioto's Study of Malnutrition

Rapid population growth has resulted in a worldwide food problem. Only a few years ago, many population and agriculture experts were concerned about whether enough food could be grown to support the world's growing population. However, recent genetic developments in cereal crops—the so-called green revolution (see Brown 1970)—have greatly increased the potential for crop production. It appears that world-wide famine will be postponed for at least another ten to twenty years, but a serious food problem remains. The new cereals are low in protein, and many of the world's people have diets that are already protein-deficient (Borgstrom 1969).

Recent work has shown that protein malnourishment during

the period at which the brain is growing fastest—up to about two years of age in humans—results in permanent neurological damage (Dobbing 1968). As expected from the neurological data, malnourishment also results in behavioral deficits. Barnes, Moore, Reid, and Pond (1968) showed that protein deficiency in young pigs impaired learning. Further, Mönckeberg (1968) and Stoch and Smythe (1968) found that these deficits extend to people; children who had suffered serious protein malnourishment when very young were found to score notably lower on intelligence tests than normally nourished children. On the basis of these studies, it might be expected that the ability to process information would be impaired by protein malnourishment. In fact, to the extent that basic components of information processing underlie intelligence, it might be more meaningful to look for deficits in the component processes. Cravioto and colleagues have been studying the effects of malnourishment on the ability to transform information from one code to another.

In one study (Cravioto, Gaona, and Birch 1967), the experimenter tapped out a rhythm on a table. The subjects then looked at visual patterns of dots with rhythmic spacings and attempted to choose the visual pattern that matched the rhythm of the auditory taps. Cravioto and DeLicardie (1968), in a related study, presented geometric forms to one sense modality and asked children whether that form was the same as or different from a form presented in another modality. The modalities were visual, haptic (active exploration with the hands), and kinesthetic (passive arm movement along the outline of the object). These tasks are different from any we have discussed previously, but they also measure the ability to transform information from one code to another.

Preliminary work by Cravioto had indicated that the height of six- to ten-year-old children from rural areas of Mexico and Guatemala correlated with malnutrition in earlier childhood. In urban areas, however, infant nutrition was better, and height was not found to be an indication of childhood malnutrition. The researchers found that shorter rural children performed worse on all transformation tasks than did taller rural children. Urban children showed no differences as a function of height. The studies indicate, therefore, that early malnutrition may permanently impair a person's information processing ability, or at least the ability to transform information from one code to another. Judging from studies of animals, most of the impairment is probably due to lack of protein rather than to a general caloric deficit.

People living in the modern world are faced with many social and environmental stresses—polluted air, noise, population density, boring jobs, malnutrition, and so on. Often these stresses result in no discernible effects on health, yet they may still impair mental efficiency. Even when there are severe health problems, as with malnutrition, people may appear to recover once the stress is remedied, but an impairment of mental abilities may persist. Information processing tasks may be an important and sensitive technique for assessing behavioral effects of environmental and population pressures.

The study of information processing is relatively new. It has undergone rapid growth only in the last twenty years, and many of the more interesting developments have occurred in the last five to ten years. Certainly, much is left to be discovered. Since it is such a new field, there have not yet been many applications of the findings. Perhaps the most extensive current applications are in the area of machine and equipment design, since the fields of information processing and human engineering share some of the same investigators. Information processing may also be useful in improving the learning of skills, in assessing environmental problems, and in gaining a new perspective on man's interaction with the world around him, including the urban environment. Another promising field is that of individual differences. As is quite apparent, there are vast differences in mental and physical abilities among different people. Some people are good artists; some are good athletes; some are skilled typists; some are brilliant mathematicians. These differences are due in part to differing interests and motivations, but they are undoubtedly also due in part to differing capacities in the various information processing tasks. Techniques for assessing information processing capacities may be an important tool for understanding individual differences.

 **REFERENCES**

Adelson, M., Muckler, F. A., and Williams, A. C., Jr. 1955. Verbal learning and message variables related to amount of information. *Information theory in psychology*, ed. H. Quastler. Glencoe, Ill.: Free Press.

Anisfeld, M., and Knapp, M. E. 1968. Association, synonymity, and directionality in false recognition. *Journal of Experimental Psychology* 77: 171-79.

Archer, E. J. 1954. Identification of visual patterns as a function of information load. *Journal of Experimental Psychology* 48: 313-17.

Attneave, F. 1959. *Applications of information theory to psychology.* New York: Holt.

Attneave, F., and Benson, B. 1969. Spatial coding of tactual stimulation. *Journal of Experimental Psychology* 81: 216-22.

Atwood, G. E. 1969. Experimental studies of mnemonic visualization. Ph.D. dissertation, University of Oregon.

———. 1971. An experimental study of visual imagination and memory. *Cognitive Psychology* 2: 290-99.

Averbach, E. 1963. The span of apprehension as a function of exposure duration. *Journal of Verbal Learning and Verbal Behavior* 2: 60-64.

Averbach, E., and Sperling, G. 1961. Short-term storage of information in vision. In *Information theory*, ed. C. Cherry, pp. 196-211. London: Butterworth.

Barclay, J. R. 1970. Noncategorical perception of a voiced stop consonant. *Proc. 78th Annual Convention, American Psychological Association.* pp. 9-10.

Barnes, R. H., Moore, A. U., Reid, I. M., and Pond, W. G. 1968. Effects of food deprivation on behavior patterns. In *Malnutrition, learning, and behavior*, ed. N. S. Scrimshaw and J. E. Gordon. Cambridge, Mass.: M.I.T. Press.

Beh, H. C., and Barratt, P. E. H. 1965. Discrimination and conditioning during sleep as indicated by the electroencephalogram. *Science* 147: 1470-71.

Berger, R. J. 1970. Sleep unease and dreams: Morpheus descending. *Psychology Today* 4: 33.

Berkeley, G. 1897. A treatise concerning the principles of human knowledge. In *The works of George Berkeley, D.D.* Vol. 1. Edited by George Sampson. London: George Bell and Sons.

Berlyne, D. E. 1957. Conflict and choice time. *British Journal of Psychology* 48: 106-18.

Bertelson, P. 1963. S-R relationships and reaction times to new versus repeated signals in a serial task. *Journal of Experimental Psychology* 65: 478-84.

———. 1967. The time course of preparation. *Quarterly Journal of Experimental Psychology* 19: 272-79.

Bertelson, P., and Tisseyre, F. 1968. The time-course of preparation with regular and irregular foreperiods. *Quarterly Journal of Experimental Psychology* 20: 297–300.

Biederman, I., and Checkosky, S. F. 1970. Processing redundant information. *Journal of Experimental Psychology* 83; 486–90.

Biederman, I., and Kaplan, R. 1970. Stimulus discriminability and S-R compatibility: Evidence for independent effects in choice reaction time. *Journal of Experimental Psychology* 86: 434–39.

Binet, A. 1890. La Concurrence des états psychologiques. *Revue Philosophique de la France et de l'étranger* 24: 138–55.

Bliss, C. B. 1892–93. Investigations in reaction time and attention. *Studies from the Yale Psychological Laboratory* 1: 1–55.

Bliss, J. C., Crane, H. D., Mansfield, K., and Townsend, J. T. 1966. Information available in brief tactile presentations. *Perception and Psychophysics* 1: 273–83.

Boder, D. P. 1935. The influence of concomitant activity and fatigue upon certain forms of reciprocal hand movement and its fundamental components. *Comparative Psychology Monographs* vol. 11,kno. 4.

Borgstrom, G. 1969. *Too many: A study of earth's biological limitations.* Toronto, Ontario: Macmillan.

Bossom, J., and Ommaya, A. K. 1968. Visuo-motor adaptation (to prismatic transformation of the retinal image) in monkeys with bilateral dorsal rhizotomy. *Brain* 91: 161–72.

Bower, G. H. 1970. Analysis of a mnemonic device. *American Scientist* 58: 496–510.

Brainard, R. W., Irby, T. S., Fitts, P. M., and Alluisi, E. A. 1962. Some variables influencing the rate of gain of information. *Journal of Experimental Psychology* 63: 105 10.

Broadbent, D. E. 1957. A mechanical model for human attention and immediate memory. *Psychological Review* 64: 205–15.

——— . 1958. *Perception and communication.* New York: Pergamon.

Brooks, L. R. 1967. The suppression of visualization by reading. *Quarterly Journal of Experimental Psychology* 19: 289–99.

——— . 1968. Spatial and verbal components of the act of recall. *Canadian Journal of Psychology* 22: 349–68.

Brown, J. 1958. Some tests of the decay theory of immediate memory. *Quarterly Journal of Experimental Psychology* 10: 12–21.

Brown, J. S., and Slater-Hammel, A. T. 1949. Discrete movements in the horizontal plane as a function of their length and direction. *Journal of Experimental Psychology* 39: 84–95.

Brown, L. R. 1970. *Seeds of change.* New York, N.Y.: Praeger Publishers.

Brown, R. W., and Lenneberg, E. H. 1958. Studies in linguistic relativity. In *Readings in social psychology*, ed. E. E. Maccoby, T. M. Newcomb, and E. L. Hartley. New York: Holt.

Brown, R. W., and McNeill, D. 1966. The "tip of the tongue" phenomenon. *Journal of Verbal Learning and Verbal Behavior* 5: 325–37.

Bruner, J. S. 1968. *Processes of cognitive growth: Infancy.* Worcester, Mass.: Clark Univ. Press.

Bugelski, B. R., Kidd, E. K., and Segman, J. 1968. The image as a mediator in one-trial paired associate learning. *Journal of Experimental Psychology* 76: 69–73.

Cherry, E. C. 1953. Some experiments on the recognition of speech, with one and with two ears. *Journal of the Acoustical Society of America* 25: 975–79.

Conrad, R. 1964. Acoustic confusions in immediate memory. *British Journal of Psychology* 55: 75–84.

——— . 1970. Short-term memory processes in the deaf. *British Journal of Psychology* 61: 179–95.

——— . 1971. The chronology of the development of covert speech in children. *Developmental Psychology* 5: 398–405.

Conrad, R., and Hull, A. J. 1968. The preferred layout for numeral data-entry keysets. *Ergonomics* 11: 165–73.

Conrad, R., and Longman, D. J. A. 1965. Standard typewriter versus chord keyboard: An experimental comparison *Ergonomics* 8: 77–88.

Conrad, R., and Rush, M. L. 1965. On the nature of short-term memory encoding by the deaf. *Journal of Speech and Hearing Disorders* 30: 336–43.

Consumer Reports. 1970. Sleeping students don't learn English. 35: 33.

Cook, J. O. 1963. "Superstition" in the Skinnerian. *American Psychologist* 18: 516–18.

Corkin, S. 1968. Acquisition of motor skill after bilateral medial temporal lobe excision. *Neuropsychologia* 6: 255–65.

Craik, F. I. M. 1971. Age differences in recognition memory. *Quarterly Journal of Experimental Psychology* 23: 316–23.

Craik, F. I. M., and Levy, B. A. 1970. Semantic and acoustic information in primary memory. *Journal of Experimental Psychology* 86: 77–82.

Cravioto, J., and DeLicardie, E. R. 1968. Intersensory development of school-age children. In *Malnutrition, learning, and behavior*, ed. N. S. Scrimshaw and J. E. Gordon. Cambridge, Mass.: M.I.T. Press.

Cravioto, J., Goana, C. E., and Birch, H. G. 1967. Early malnutrition and auditory-visual integration in school-age children. *Journal of Special Education* 2: 75–82.

Crossman, E. R. F. W. 1955. The measurement of discriminability. *Quarterly Journal of Experimental Psychology* 7: 176–95.

Crossman, E. R. F. W., and Goodeve, P. J. 1963. Feedback control of hand-movement and Fitts' Law. In *Proceedings of the Experimental Society.* Oxford.

Crowder, R. G. 1967. Short-term memory for words with perceptual-motor interpolated activity. *Journal of Verbal Learning and Verbal Behavior* 6: 753–61.

Crowder, R. G., and Morton, J. 1969. Precategorical acoustic storage (PAS). *Perception and Psychophysics* 5: 365–73.

Dallett, K. M. 1964. Number of categories and category information in free recall. *Journal of Experimental Psychology* 68: 1–12.

Dawes, R. M. 1964. Cognitive distortion. *Psychological Reports* 14: 443–59.

——— . 1966. Memory and distortion of meaningful written material. *British Journal of Psychology* 57: 77–86.

Deutsch, J. A., and Deutsch, D. 1963. Attention: Some theoretical considerations. *Psychological Review* 70: 80–90.

Dobbing, J. 1968. Effects of experimental undernutrition on development of the nervous system. In *Malnutrition, learning, and behavior*, ed. N. S. Scrimshaw and J. C. Gordon. Cambridge, Mass.: M.I.T. Press.

Donders, F. C. 1969. On the speed of mental processes. Trans. W. G. Koster. In *Attention and performance II*, ed. W. G. Koster. Amsterdam: North-Holland Publishing Co.

Eagle, M., and Leiter, E. 1964. Recall and recognition in intentional and incidental learning. *Journal of Experimental Psychology* 68: 58–63.

Egeth, H., and Pachella, R. 1969. Multidimensional stimulus identification. *Perception and Psychophysics* 5: 341–46.

Eichelman, W. H. 1970. Stimulus and response repetition effects for naming letters at two response-stimulus intervals. *Perception and Psychophysics* 7: 94–96.

Eimas, P. D., Siqueland, E. R., Jusczyk, P., and Vigorito, J. 1971. Speech perception in infants. *Science* 171: 303–6.

Ells, J. G. 1969. Attentional requirements of movement control. Ph.D. dissertation, University of Oregon.

Emmons, W. H., and Simon, C. W. 1956. The non-recall of material presented during sleep. *American Journal of Psychology* 69: 76–81.

Eriksen, C. W., and Collins, J. F. 1968. Sensory traces versus the psychological moment in the temporal organization of form. *Journal of Experimental Psychology* 77: 376–82.

Eriksen, C. W., and Hake, H. W. 1955. Absolute judgments as a function of stimulus range and number of stimulus and response categories. *Journal of Experimental Psychology* 49: 323–32.

Eriksen, C. W., and Johnson, H. J. 1964. Storage and decay characteristics of nonattended auditory stimuli. *Journal of Experimental Psychology* 8: 28–36.

Festinger, L., Ono, H., Burnham, C. A., and Bamber, D. 1967. Efference and the conscious experience of perception. *Journal of Experimental Psychology* 74: Monograph no. 2, pt. 2.

Fitts, P. M. 1954. The information capacity of the human motor system in controlling the amplitude of movement. *Journal of Experimental Psychology* 47: 381–91.

Fitts, P. M., and Jones, R. E. 1961. Analysis of factors contributing to 460 "pilot-error" experiences in operating aircraft controls. In *Selected papers on human factors in the design and use of control systems*, ed. H. W. Sinaiko. New York: Dover.

Fitts, P. M., and Peterson, J. R. 1964. Information capacity of discrete motor responses. *Journal of Experimental Psychology* 67: 103–12.

Fitts, P. M., Peterson, J. R., and Wolpe, G. 1963. Cognitive aspects of information processing: II. Adjustments to stimulus redundancy. *Journal of Experimental Psychology* 65: 423–32.

Fitts, P. M., and Seeger, C. M. 1953. SR compatibility: Spatial characteristics of stimulus and response codes. *Journal of Experimental Psychology* 46: 199–210.

Flavell, J. H., Friedrichs, A. G., and Hoyt, J. D. 1970. Developmental changes in memorization processes. *Cognitive Psychology* 1: 324–40.

Fleishman, E. A., and Rich, S. 1963. Role of kinesthetic and spatial-visual abilities in perceptual-motor learning. *Journal of Experimental Psychology* 66: 6–11.

Fogel, L. J. 1963. *Biotechnology: Concepts and applications.* Englewood Cliffs, N.J.: Prentice-Hall.

Garner, W. R. 1962. *Uncertainty and structure as psychological concepts.* New York: Wiley.

Garner, W. R., and Felfoldy, G. L. 1970. Integrality of stimulus dimensions in various types of information processing. *Cognitive Psychology* 1: 225–41.

Gibbs, C. B. 1970. Servo-control systems in organisms and the transfer of skill. In *Skills*, ed. D. Legge. Middlesex: Penguin.

Gottsdanker, R., Broadbent, L., and Van Sant, C. 1963. Reaction time to single and to first signals. *Journal of Experimental Psychology* 66: 163–67.

Gottsdanker, R., and Stelmach, G. E. 1971. The persistence of psychological refractoriness. *Journal of Motor Behavior* 3: 301–12.

Greenwald, A. G. 1970. Sensory feedback mechanisms in performance control: With special reference to the ideo-motor mechanism. *Psychological Review* 77: 73–99.

Grosser, G. S., and Siegal, A. W. 1971. Emergence of a tonic-phasic model for sleep and dreaming. *Psychological Bulletin* 75: 60–72.

Grossman, L., and Eagle, M. 1970. Synonymity, antonymity, and association in false recognition responses. *Journal of Experimental Psychology* 83: 244–48.

Hailman, J. P. 1969. How an instinct is learned. *Scientific American* 221: 98–106.

Hawkins, H. L. 1969. Parallel processing in complex visual discrimination. *Perception and Psychophysics* 5: 56–64.

Hawkins, H. L., Thomas, G. B., and Drury, K. B. 1970. Perceptual versus response bias in discrete choice reaction time. *Journal of Experimental Psychology* 84: 514–17.

Hefferline, R. F., Keenan, B., and Harford, R. A. 1959. Escape and avoidance conditioning in human subjects without their observation of response. *Science* 130: 1338–39.

Hellyer, S. 1963. Stimulus-response coding and amount of information as determinants of reaction time. *Journal of Experimental Psychology* 65: 521–22.

Hershberger, W. A., and Terry, D. F. 1965. Typographical cuing in conventional and programmed texts. *Journal of Applied Psychology* 49: 55–60.

Hick, W. E. 1952. On the rate of gain of information. *Quarterly Journal of Experimental Psychology* 4: 11–26.

Hinde, R. A. 1969. Control of movement patterns in animals. *Quarterly Journal of Experimental Psychology* 21: 105–26.

Hinrichs, J. V., and Krainz, P. L. 1970. Expectancy in choice reaction time: Anticipation of stimulus or response? *Journal of Experimental Psychology* 85: 330–34.

Hintzman, D. L. 1965. Classification and aural coding in short-term memory. *Psychonomic Science* 3: 161–62.

Hintzman, D. L., et al. "Stroop" effect: Input or output phenomenon? *Journal of Experimental Psychology* 95: 458–59.

Hockey, G. R. J. 1970a. Effect of loud noise on attentional selectivity. *Quarterly Journal of Experimental Psychology* 22: 28–36.

————. 1970b. Signal probability and spatial location as possible bases for increased selectivity in noise. *Quarterly Journal of Experimental Psychology* 22: 37–42.

Holding, D. H. 1965. *Principles of training.* New York: Pergamon.

Horowitz, L. M., Lampel, A. K., and Takanishi, R. N. 1969. The child's memory for unitized scenes. *Journal of Experimental Child Psychology* 8: 375–88.

Houston, B. K. 1969. Noise, task difficulty, and Stroop color-word performance. *Journal of Experimental Psychology* 82: 403–4.

Howard, I. P., and Templeton, W. B. 1966. *Human spatial orientation.* New York: Wiley.

Hyman, R. 1953. Stimulus information as a determinant of reaction time. *Journal of Experimental Psychology* 45: 188–96.

Hyman, R., and Umiltà, C. 1969. The information hypothesis and nonrepetitions. In *Attention and Performance,* vol. 2, ed. W. G. Koster, pp. 37–53. Amsterdam: North-Holland Publishing Co.

Kalikow, D. N. 1971. Information processing models and computer aids for human performance: Second language learning. Technical Report No. 2185. Cambridge, Mass.: Bolt, Beranek, and Newman.

Karlin, L., and Kestenbaum, R. 1968. Effects of number of alternatives on the psychological refractory period. *Quarterly Journal of Experimental Psychology* 20: 167–78.

Keele, S. W. 1967. Compatibility and time-sharing in serial reaction time. *Journal of Experimental Psychology* 75: 529–39.

――――. 1968. Movement control in skilled motor performance. *Psychological Bulletin* 70: 387–403.

――――. 1969. Repetition effect: A memory-dependent process. *Journal of Experimental Psychology* 80: 243–48.

――――. 1970. Effects of input and output modes on decision time. *Journal of Experimental Psychology* 85: 157–64.

――――. 1972. Attention demands of memory retrieval. *Journal of Experimental Psychology* 93: 245–48.

Keele, S. W., and Boies, S. J. 1972. Processing demands of sequential information. Paper presented at the meeting of the Western Psychological Association, Portland, Oregon, April 1972.

Keele, S. W., and Chase, W. G. 1967. Short-term visual storage. *Perception and Psychophysics* 2: 383–85.

Keele, S. W., and Ells, J. G. Memory characteristics of kinesthetic information. *Journal of Motor Behavior*, in press.

Keele, S. W., and Posner, M. I. 1968. Processing of visual feedback in rapid movements. *Journal of Experimental Psychology* 77: 155–58.

Keppel, G., and Underwood, B. J. 1962. Proactive inhibition in short-term retention of single items. *Journal of Verbal Learning and Verbal Behavior* 1: 153–61.

Kintsch, W. 1970. Recognition memory in bilingual subjects. *Journal of Verbal Learning and Verbal Behavior* 0. 405 9.

Kintsch, W., and Buschke, H. 1969. Homophones and synonyms in short-term memory. *Journal of Experimental Psychology* 80: 403–7.

Kolers, P. A. 1966. Interlingual facilitation of short-term memory. *Journal of Verbal Learning and Verbal Behavior* 5: 314–19.

Konishi, M. 1965. The role of auditory feedback in the control of vocalization in the white-crowned sparrow. *Z. Tierpsychologie* 22: 770–83.

Kornblum, S. 1969. Sequential determinants of information processing in serial and discrete choice reaction time. *Psychological Review* 76: 113–31.

Laabs, G. J. 1971. Cue effects in motor short-term memory. Ph.D. dissertation, University of Oregon.

LaBerge, D., and Tweedy, J. R. 1964. Presentation probability and choice time. *Journal of Experimental Psychology* 68: 477–81.

LaBerge, D., Van Gelder, P., and Yellott, J., Jr. 1970. A cueing technique in choice reaction time. *Perception and Psychophysics* 7: 57–62.

Lashley, K. S. 1951. The problem of serial order in behavior. In *Cerebral mechanisms in behavior: The Hixon symposium*, ed. L. A. Jeffress. New York: Wiley.

Laurence, M. W., and Trotter, M. 1971. Effect of acoustic factors and list organization in multitrial free recall learning of college age and elderly adults. *Developmental Psychology* 5: 202–10.

Lazlo, J. I. 1966. The performance of a simple motor task with kinaesthetic sense loss. *Quarterly Journal of Experimental Psychology* 18: 1–8.

————. 1967. Training of fast tapping with reduction of kinaesthetic, tactile, visual and auditory sensations. *Quarterly Journal of Experimental Psychology* 19: 344–49.

Leonard, J. A. 1959. Tactual choice reactions. *Quarterly Journal of Experimental Psychology* 11: 76–83.

Lewis, J. L. 1970. Semantic processing of unattended messages using dichotic listening. *Journal of Experimental Psychology* 85: 225–28.

Lewis, J., Baddeley, A. D., Bonham, K. G., and Lovett, D. 1970. Traffic pollution and mental efficiency. *Nature* 225: 95–97.

Liberman, A. M., Cooper, F. S., Shankweiler, D. P., and Studdert-Kennedy, M. 1967. Perception of the speech code. *Psychological Review* 74: 431–61.

Locke, J. 1813. *An essay concerning human understanding: Book II.* Boston: Cummings, Hilliard, and Buckingham.

Locke, J. L., and Locke, V. L. 1971. Deaf children's phonetic, visual, and dactylic coding in a grapheme recall task. *Journal of Experimental Psychology* 89: 142–46.

Luria, A. R. 1968. *The mind of a mnemonist.* Trans. Lynn Solotaroff. New York: Basic Books.

Mackworth, J. F. 1963. The duration of the visual image. *Canadian Journal of Psychology* 17: 62–81.

McLaughlin, S. C. 1967. Parametric adjustment in saccadic eye movements. *Perception and Psychophysics* 2: 359–62.

Marler, P. R., and Hamilton, W. S., III. 1966. *Mechanisms of animal behavior.* New York: Wiley.

Melton, A. W. 1963. Implications of short-term memory for a general theory of memory. *Journal of Verbal Learning and Verbal Behavior* 2: 1–21.

Milgram, S. 1970. The experience of living in cities. *Science* 167: 1461–68.

Miller, G. A. 1956. The magical number seven plus or minus two: Some limits on our capacity for processing information. *Psychological Review* 63: 81–97.

Miller, G. A., and Selfridge, J. A. 1950. Verbal context and the recall of meaningful material. *American Journal of Psychology* 63: 176–85.

Milner, B., Corkin, S., and Teuber, H. L. 1968. Further analysis of the hippocampal amnesic syndrome: 14-year follow-up of H. M. *Neuropsychologia* 6: 215–34.

Mönckeberg, F. 1968. Effects of early malnutrition on subsequent physical and psychological development. In *Malnutrition, learning, and behavior,* ed. N. S. Scrimshaw and J. E. Gordon. Cambridge, Mass.: M.I.T. Press.

Montgomery, J. M. 1971. Intervening task and delay effects in motor STM. Paper presented at the Third Canadian Psycho-Motor Learning and Sport Psychology Symposium, Vancouver, B.C.

Moray, N. 1959. Attention in dichotic listening: Affective cues and the influence of instructions. *Quarterly Journal of Experimental Psychology* 11: 56–60.

Morgan, B. B., and Alluisi, E. A. 1967. Effects of discriminability and irrelevant information on absolute judgments. *Perception and Psychophysics* 2: 54–58.

Morgan, C. T., Cook, J. S., III, Chapanis, A., and Lund, M. W., eds. 1963. *Human engineering guide to equipment design.* New York: McGraw-Hill.

Morin, R. E., and Forrin, B. 1963. Response equivocation and reaction time. *Journal of Experimental Psychology* 66: 30–36.

Morton, J. 1969a. Interaction of information in word recognition. *Psychological Review* 76: 165-78.

———. 1969b. The use of correlated stimulus information in card sorting. *Perception and Psychophysics* 5: 374-76.

Mott, F. W., and Sherrington, C. S. 1895. Experiments upon the influence of sensory nerves upon movement and nutrition of the limbs: Preliminary communication. *Proceedings of the Royal Society of London* 57: 481-88.

Mowbray, G. H. 1960. Choice reaction time for skilled responses. *Quarterly Journal of Experimental Psychology* 12: 193-202.

Mowbray, G. H., and Rhoades, M. U. 1959. On the reduction of choice-reaction times with practice. *Quarterly Journal of Experimental Psychology* 11: 16-23.

Murdock, B. B., Jr. 1961. The retention of individual items. *Journal of Experimental Psychology* 62: 618-25.

Murray, D. J. 1968. Articulation and acoustic confusability in short-term memory. *Journal of Experimental Psychology* 78: 679-84.

Nazzaro, J. R., and Nazzaro, J. N. 1970. Auditory versus visual learning of temporal patterns. *Journal of Experimental Psychology* 84: 477-78.

Neimark, E., Slotnick, N. S., and Ulrich, T. 1971. Development of memorization strategies. *Developmental Psychology* 5: 427-32.

Neisser, U. 1967. *Cognitive Psychology*. New York: Appleton-Century-Crofts.

Niebel, B. W. 1962. *Motion and time study*. Homewood, Ill.: Irwin.

Norman, D. A. 1968. Toward a theory of memory and attention. *Psychological Review* 75: 522-36.

Nottebohm, F. 1970. Ontogeny of bird song. *Science* 167: 950-56.

Notterman, J. M., and Page, D. E. 1962. Evaluation of mathematically equivalent tracking systems. *Perceptual and Motor Skills* 15: 683-716.

Oswald, I. 1966. *Sleep*. Baltimore: Penguin.

Peterson, L. R., Hillner, K., and Saltzman, D. 1962. Supplementary report: Time between pairings and short-term retention. *Journal of Experimental Psychology* 64: 550-51.

Peterson, L. R., and Peterson, M. 1959. Short-term retention of individual items. *Journal of Experimental Psychology* 58: 193-98.

Pew, R. W. 1966. Acquisition of hierarchical control over the temporal organization of a skill. *Journal of Experimental Psychology* 71: 764-71.

Pollack, I. 1952. The information of elementary auditory displays, I. *Journal of the Acoustical Society of America* 24: 745-49.

Pompi, K. F., and Lachman, R. 1967. Surrogate processes in the short-term retention of connected discourse. *Journal of Experimental Psychology* 75: 143-50.

Posner, M. I. 1964a. Information reduction in the analysis of sequential tasks. *Psychological Review* 71: 491-504.

———. 1964b. Rate of presentation and order of recall in immediate memory. *British Journal of Psychology* 55: 303-6.

———. 1967. Characteristics of visual and kinesthetic memory codes. *Journal of Experimental Psychology* 75: 103-7.

———. 1969. Reduced attention and the performance of "automated" movements. *Journal of Motor Behavior* 1: 245-58.

———. 1970. On the relationship between letter names and superordinate categories. *Quarterly Journal of Experimental Psychology* 22: 279-89.

Posner, M. I., and Boies, S. J. 1971. Components of attention. *Psychological Review* 78: 391-408.

Posner, M. I., Boies, S. J., Eichelman, W. H., and Taylor, R. L. 1969. Retention of visual and name codes of single letters. *Journal of Experimental Psychology Monograph* 79: 1–16.

Posner, M. I., Buggie, S. E., and Summers, J. J. 1971. On the selection of signals. Paper presented at the meeting of the Psychomics Society, St. Louis, November 1971.

Posner, M. I., and Keele, S. W. 1968. On the genesis of abstract ideas. *Journal of Experimental Psychology* 77: 353–63.

Posner, M. I., and Keele, S. W. 1969. Attention demands of movements. *Proceedings of the Seventeenth Congress of Applied Psychology*. Amsterdam: Zeitlinger.

Posner, M. I., and Keele, S. W. 1970a. Retention of abstract ideas. *Journal of Experimental Psychology* 83: 304–8.

Posner, M. I., and Keele, S. W. 1970b. Time and space as measures of mental operations. Paper presented at the 78th Annual Convention of the American Psychological Association, Division 3, September 1970.

Posner, M. I., and Keele, S. W. 1972. Skill learning. In *Handbook of research on teaching*, ed. R. M. W. Travers. Washington, D.C.: American Educational Research Association.

Posner, M. I., and Konick, A. F. 1966. Short-term retention of visual and kinesthetic information. *Organizational Behavior and Human Performance* 1: 71–86.

Posner, M. I. and Mitchell, R. 1967. A chronometric analysis of classification. *Psychological Review* 74: 392–409.

Posner, M. I., and Rossman, E. 1965. Effect of size and location of informational transforms upon short-term retention. *Journal of Experimental Psychology* 70: 496–505.

Pronko, N. H. 1969. On learning to play the violin at the age of four without tears. *Psychology Today* 2: 52.

Rabbitt, P. M. 1967. Signal discriminability, S-R compatibility and choice reaction time. *Psychonomics Science* 7: 419–20.

Reed, S. K. 1970. Decision processes in pattern classification. Ph.D. dissertation, University of California, Los Angeles.

Reicher, G. M. 1969. Perceptual recognition as a function of meaningfulness of stimulus material. *Journal of Experimental Psychology* 81: 275–80.

Reynolds, D. 1966. Time and event uncertainty in unisensory reaction time. *Journal of Experimental Psychology* 71: 286–93.

Rundus, D. 1971. Analysis of rehearsal processes in free recall. *Journal of Experimental Psychology* 89: 63–77.

Sanders, A. F. 1970. Some variables affecting the relation between relative stimulus frequency and choice reaction time. In *Attention and Performance, III*, ed. A. F. Sanders. Amsterdam: North-Holland Publishing Co.

Schvaneveldt, R. W. 1969. Effects of complexity in simultaneous reaction time tasks. *Journal of Experimental Psychology* 81: 289–96.

Schvaneveldt, R. W., and Chase, W. G. 1969. Sequential effects in choice reaction time. *Journal of Experimental Psychology* 80: 1–8.

Schvaneveldt, R. W., and Staudenmayer, H. 1970. Mental arithmetic and the uncertainty effect in choice reaction time. *Journal of Experimental Psychology* 85: 111–17.

Seibel, R. 1963. Discrimination reaction time for a 1,023 alternative task. *Journal of Experimental Psychology* 66: 215–26.

Shallice, T., and Warrington, E. K. 1970. Independent functioning of verbal memory stores: A neuropsychological study. *Quarterly Journal of Experimental Psychology* 22: 261–73.

Shannon, C. E., and Weaver, W. 1949. *The mathematical theory of communication.* Urbana, Ill.: Univ. of Illinois Press.

Shepard, R. N. 1967. Recognition memory for words, sentences, and pictures. *Journal of Verbal Learning and Verbal Behavior* 6: 156–63.

Shepard, R. N., and Sheenan, M. M. 1965. Immediate recall of numbers containing a familiar prefix or postfix. *Perceptual and Motor Skills.* 21: 263–73.

Simon, C. W., and Emmons, W. H. 1956. Responses to material presented during various levels of sleep. *Journal of Experimental Psychology* 51: 89–97.

Smith, E. E. 1968. Choice reaction time: An analysis of the major theoretical positions. *Psychological Bulletin* 69: 77–110.

Smith, M. C. 1967. Theories of the psychological refractory period. *Psychological Bulletin* 67: 202–13.

———. 1968. Repetition effect and short-term memory. *Journal of Experimental Psychology* 77: 435–39.

Sperling, G. 1960. The information available in brief visual presentations. *Psychological Monographs,* vol. 74.

———. 1963. A Model for verbal memory tasks. *Human Factors* 5: 19–31.

Spieth, W., Curtis, J. F., and Webster, J. C. 1954. Responding to one of two simultaneous messages. *Journal of the Acoustical Society of America* 26: 391–96.

Sternberg, S. 1969. The discovery of processing stages: Extensions of Donders' method. In *Attention and Performance,* vol. 2, ed. W. G. Koster. Amsterdam: North-Holland Publishing Co.

Stoch, N. B., and Smythe, P. M. 1968. Undernutrition during infancy, and subsequent brain growth and intellectual development. In *Malnutrition, learning, and behavior,* ed. N. S. Scrimshaw and J. E. Gordon. Cambridge, Mass.: M.I.T. Press.

Stone, M. 1960. Models for choice-reaction time. *Psychometrika* 25: 251–60.

Strange, W., Keeney, T., Kessel, F. S., and Jenkins, J. J. 1970. Abstraction over time of prototypes from distortions of random dot patterns. *Journal of Experimental Psychology* 83. 508–10.

Swets, J. A. 1961. Is there a sensory threshold? *Science* 134: 168–77.

Talland, G. 1967. Amnesia: A world without continuity. *Psychology Today* 1: 43–50.

Taub, E., and Berman, A. J. 1968. Movement and learning in the absence of sensory feedback. In *The neuropsychology of spatially oriented behavior,* ed. S. J. Freedman. Homewood, Ill.: Dorsey.

Toffler, A. 1970. *Future shock.* New York: Bantam.

Treisman, A. M. 1964. Monitoring and storage of irrelevant messages in selective attention. *Journal of Verbal Learning and Verbal Behavior* 3: 449–59.

———. 1971. Shifting attention between ears. *Quarterly Journal of Experimental Psychology* 23: 157–67.

Tulving, E. 1962. Subjective organization in free recall of "unrelated" words. *Psychological Review* 69: 344–54.

———. 1966. Subjective organization and effects of repetition in multitrial free-recall learning. *Journal of Verbal Learning and Verbal Behavior* 5: 193–97.

Turnbull, E. R. S. 1971. Visual and name processes in a visual search task. Master's thesis, University of Oregon.

Uhr, L., and Vossler, C. 1963. A pattern-recognition program that generates, evaluates, and adjusts its own operators. In *Com-*

puters and thought, ed. E. A. Feigenbaum and J. Feldman. New York: McGraw-Hill.

Umiltà, C., and Trombini, G. 1968. La distribuzione delle probabilità degli stimoli come fattore determinante nei tempi di reazione a scelta multipla. *Rivista di Psicologia,* Fascicola Speciale, pp. 91–98.

Underwood, B. J. 1965. False recognition produced by implicit verbal responses. *Journal of Experimental Psychology* 70: 122–29.

Vince, M. A. 1948. Corrective movements in a pursuit task. *Quarterly Journal of Experimental Psychology* 1: 85–103.

Wallace, W. P., and Calderone, R. N. 1969. Implicit responses in incidental learning. *Journal of Verbal Learning and Verbal Behavior* 8: 136–42.

Warrington, E. K., and Shallice, T. 1972. Neuropsychological evidence of visual storage in short-term memory tasks. *Quarterly Journal of Experimental Psychology* 24: 30–40.

Watson, J. B. 1924. *Behaviorism.* New York: People's Institute.

Waugh, N. C. 1969. Free recall of conspicuous items. *Journal of Verbal Learning and Verbal Behavior* 8: 448–56.

Waugh, N. C., and Norman, D. A. 1965. Primary memory. *Psychological Review* 72: 89–104.

Weinberg, H. 1966. Evidence suggesting the acquisition of a simple discrimination during sleep. *Canadian Journal of Psychology* 20: 1–11.

Welch, J. C. 1898. On the measurement of mental activity through muscular activity and the determination of a constant of attention. *American Journal of Physiology* 1: 253–306.

Welford, A. T. 1960. The measurement of sensory-motor performance: Survey and reappraisal of twelve years' progress. *Ergonomics* 3: 189–230.

Well, A. D. 1971. The influence of irrelevant information on speeded classification tasks. *Perception and Psychophysics* 10: 79–84.

Whorf, B. L. 1940. Science and linguistics. *Technology Review* 44: 229–31, 247–48.

Wickelgren, W. A. 1966. Consolidation and retroactive interference in short-term recognition memory for pitch. *Journal of Experimental Psychology* 72: 250–59.

———. 1968. Sparing of short-term memory in an amnesic patient: Implications for strength theory of memory. *Neuropsychologia* 6: 235–44.

Wilkinson, R. T. 1963. Interaction of noise with knowledge of results and sleep deprivation. *Journal of Experimental Psychology* 66: 332–37.

Wilkinson, R. T., and Colquhoun, W. P. 1968. Interaction of alcohol with incentive and with sleep deprivation. *Journal of Experimental Psychology* 76: 623–29.

Williams, H. L., Beaver, W. S., Spence, M. T., and Rundell, O. H. 1969. Digital and kinesthetic memory with interpolated information processing. *Journal of Experimental Psychology* 80: 530–36.

Wilson, D. M. 1961. The central nervous control of flight in a locust. *Journal of Experimental Biology* 38: 471–90.

Woodworth, R. S. 1899. The accuracy of voluntary movement. *Psychological Review,* vol. 3.

———. 1938. *Experimental psychology.* New York: Henry Holt.

Yates, F. A. 1966. *The art of memory.* Chicago: University of Chicago Press.

NAME INDEX

SUBJECT INDEX